W9-BUA-698

weird but true! 7

That's Weird!

NATIONAL GEOGRAPHIC KIDS
weird but true!
7
350 OUTRAGEOUS FACTS
NATIONAL GEOGRAPHIC
WASHINGTON, D.C.

NEW
YORKE

On average, the
Empire State Building
in New York City
is hit by
lightning
25 times
a year.

AN ITALIAN DESIGNER MADE A COUCH SHAPED LIKE A CHOCOLATE BAR.
RED-FOOTED TORTOISES HAVE BEEN TAUGHT TO USE TOUCH SCREENS.
Sitting in a cardboard box can lower stress for domestic cats.

Your brain makes up only 2 percent of your total body weight but uses up to 20 percent of your body's energy.

HONEYBEES HAVE **TWO** STOMACHS.

Some **frogs** have **green** bones.

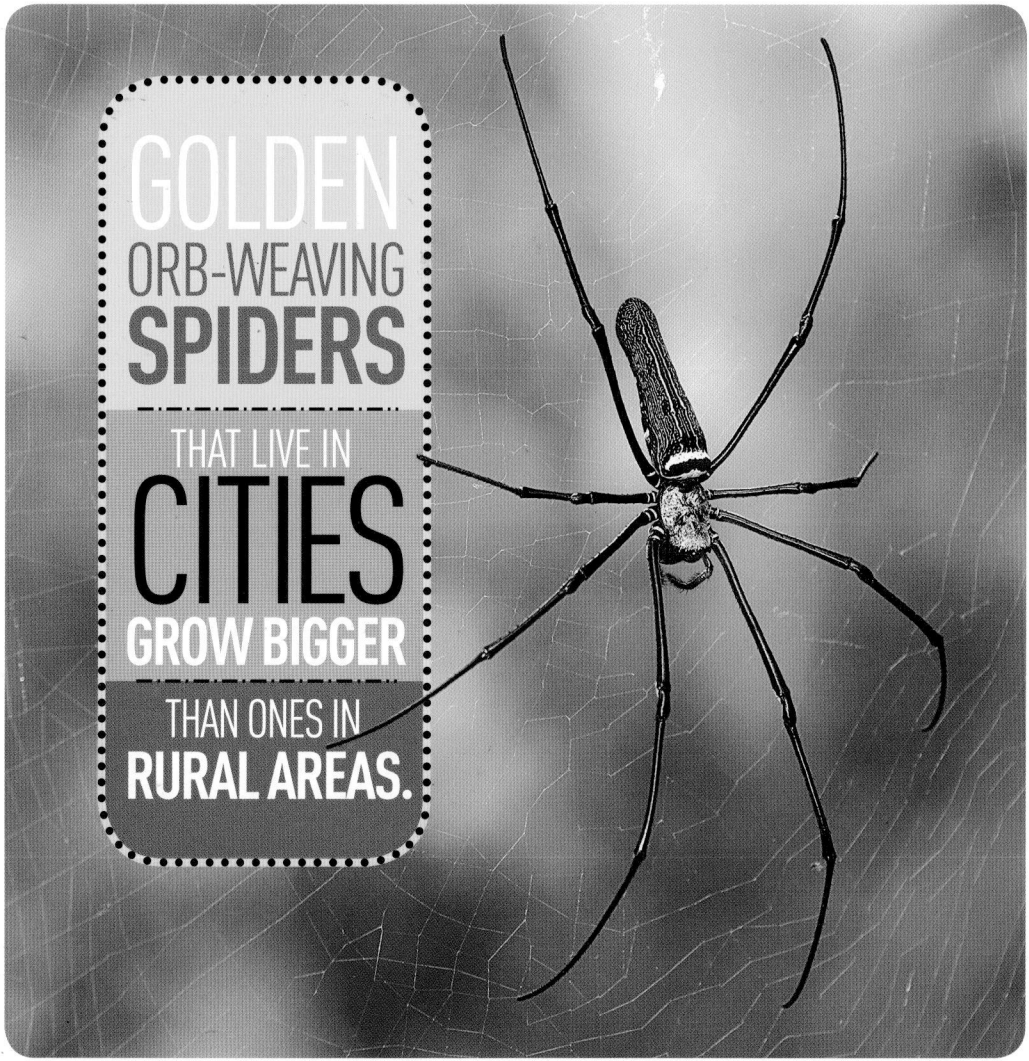
GOLDEN
ORB-WEAVING
SPIDERS
THAT LIVE IN
CITIES
GROW BIGGER
THAN ONES IN
RURAL AREAS.

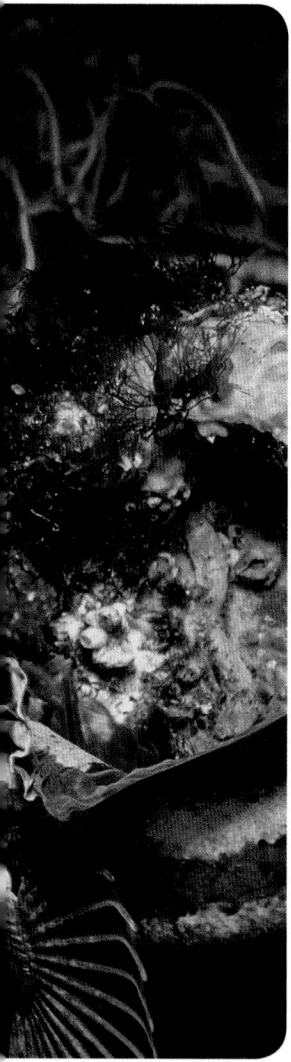

SARCASTIC FRINGEHEAD FISH BATTLE OVER TURF BY WRESTLING EACH OTHER WITH THEIR MOUTHS.

THE HEAVIEST **CAULIFLOWER** ON RECORD WEIGHED MORE **THAN A BULLDOG.**

UP TO HALF OF THE WATER ON EARTH IS OLDER THAN THE SUN, ACCORDING TO ONE STUDY.

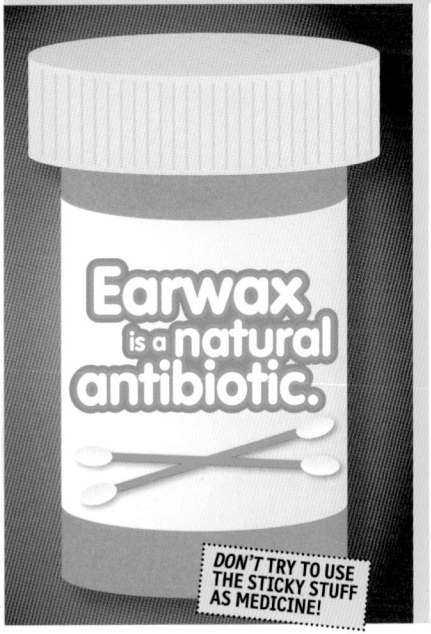

Food travels through your esophagus at a speed of about one inch (2.5 cm) a second.

A STUDY FOUND THAT **CHEWING GUM** PUTS YOU IN A **BETTER MOOD.**

ONE MAN INVENTED **A SUPERFAST POTATO PEELER** OUT OF A TOILET BRUSH ATTACHED TO A DRILL.

A
SPANISH SCIENTIST
INVENTED
ICE
CREAM
THAT
CHANGES
COLORS
WHEN
LICKED.

THE PUDU—A SMALL KIND OF DEER—RUNS IN A ZIGZAG PATTERN TO ESCAPE PREDATORS.

YOU HAVE TASTE RECEPTORS IN YOUR STOMACH.

SPITTING SPIDERS IMMOBILIZE PREY BY SPRAYING THEM WITH POISONOUS FLUID.

It takes more than ten gallons (38 L) of water to make one slice of bread.

The average wait time
at a fast-food
restaurant
drive-through is
232 seconds.

SPECIAL
VENDING MACHINES
IN ISTANBUL, TURKEY,
AUTOMATICALLY DISPENSE
FOOD AND WATER
FOR DOGS.
KARTAL BELEDİYESİ
KARTAL BELEDİYESİ
Çöpe atmayalım, Ayıralım,
Geleceğimizi Geri Kazanalım
Alo Çevre : 280 60 60
www. kartal.bel.tr
www.twitter.com/kartalbld
www.facebook.com/kartalbld
Karnım tok
keyfim yerinde
KARTAL BELEDİYESİ
Çöpe Atma
Buraya at

Cockroaches
that lived
250 million
years ago
were as big as
today's house cats.

ME-EW!

ARTIST CHARLES M. SCHULZ CREATED NEARLY 18,000 "PEANUTS" COMIC STRIPS.

Scientists have found a way to return hard-boiled egg whites to liquid form.

Some airplane pilots use a beach on Fraser Island, Australia, as a landing strip.

PASSENGERS ARRIVING AT ONE **NEW ZEALAND AIRPORT** ARE GREETED BY A **14-FOOT BUST** OF THE **DRAGON** (4.3-m) **Smaug** **FROM *THE HOBBIT*** MOVIE TRILOGY.

Scientists think that the center of the moon may be SQUISHY.

IF THE DORMANT **SUPER-VOLCANO** IN YELLOWSTONE NATIONAL PARK, U.S.A., EVER **ERUPTED,** IT WOULD LIKELY SPEW ENOUGH **ASH** TO COVER ALL OF **NORTH AMERICA.**

The Pac-Man frog can lift three times its own **body weight** with its tongue.

LISTENING TO CLASSICAL MUSIC CAN HELP DOGS RELAX, A STUDY FOUND.

A DUTCH COMPANY PLANS TO BUILD A **SNOWFLAKE-SHAPED HOTEL** THAT FLOATS ON **WATER.**

THIS IS THE DESIGN FOR THE HOTEL. COOL, HUH?

A NEWSPAPER IN SRI LANKA

was printed with insect-repelling ink to keep readers from getting bug bites.

HUMANS AND KATYDIDS

HAVE SIMILARLY STRUCTURED

EARS.

THE GIANT PITCHER PLANT SECRETES NECTAR TO LURE BUGS AND RODENTS INTO ITS "MOUTH."

A SOUTH KOREAN BASEBALL TEAM INSTALLED **CHEERING ROBOTS** IN THE STANDS OF ITS BALLPARK.

A record 232 people did a **cannonball dive** all at once into a harbor in New Zealand.

ONE KIND OF

MUSHROOM RESEMBLES A

HUMAN BRAIN.

Between 1886 and 1902, the Statue of Liberty was used as a lighthouse.

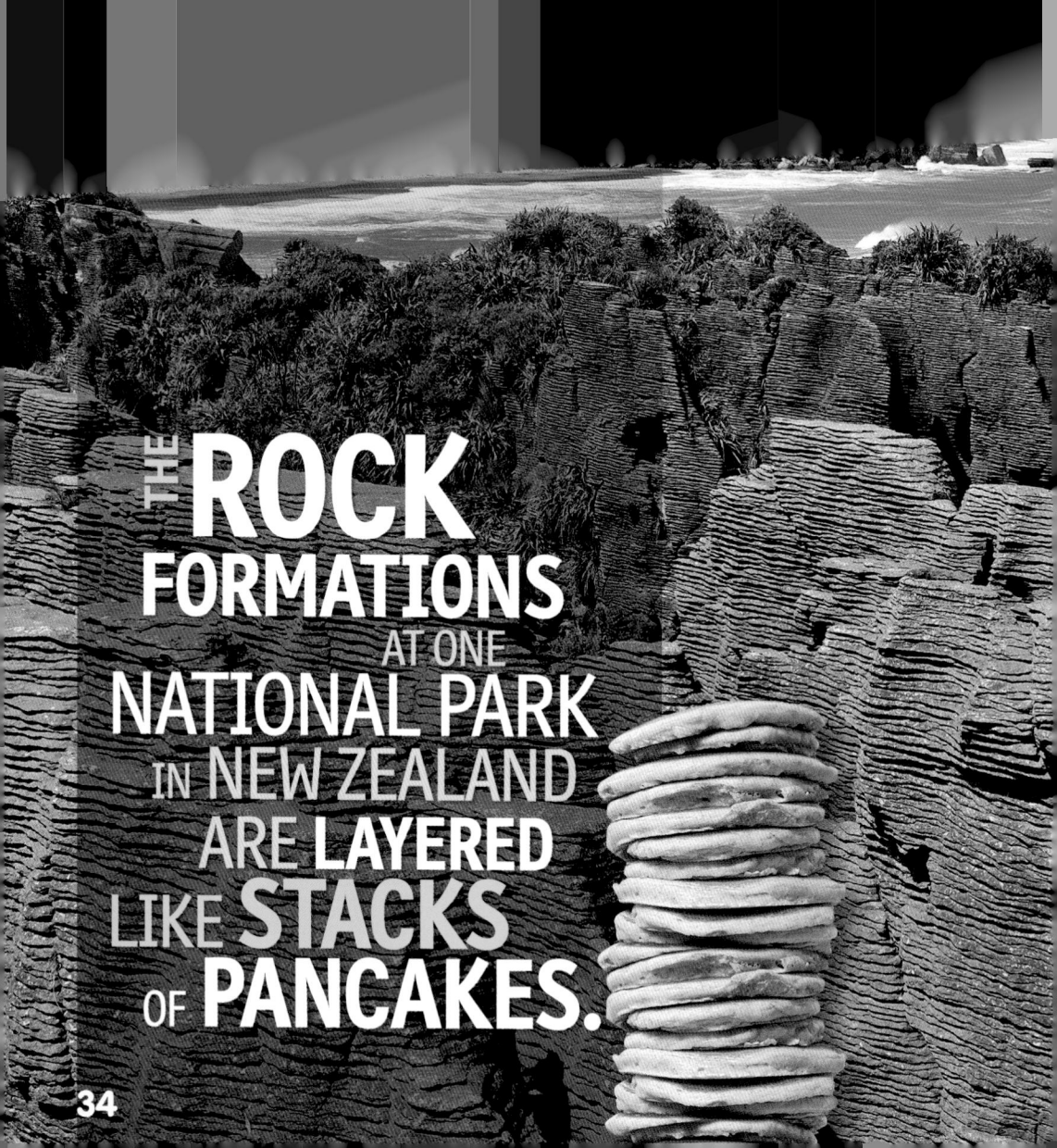

THE **ROCK FORMATIONS** AT ONE NATIONAL PARK IN NEW ZEALAND ARE **LAYERED** LIKE **STACKS** OF **PANCAKES.**

GIANT CUTTLEFISH HAVE BAGEL-SHAPED BRAINS.

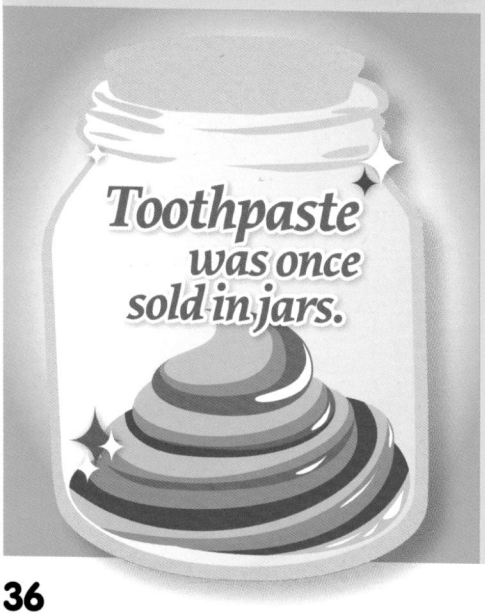
Toothpaste was once sold in jars.

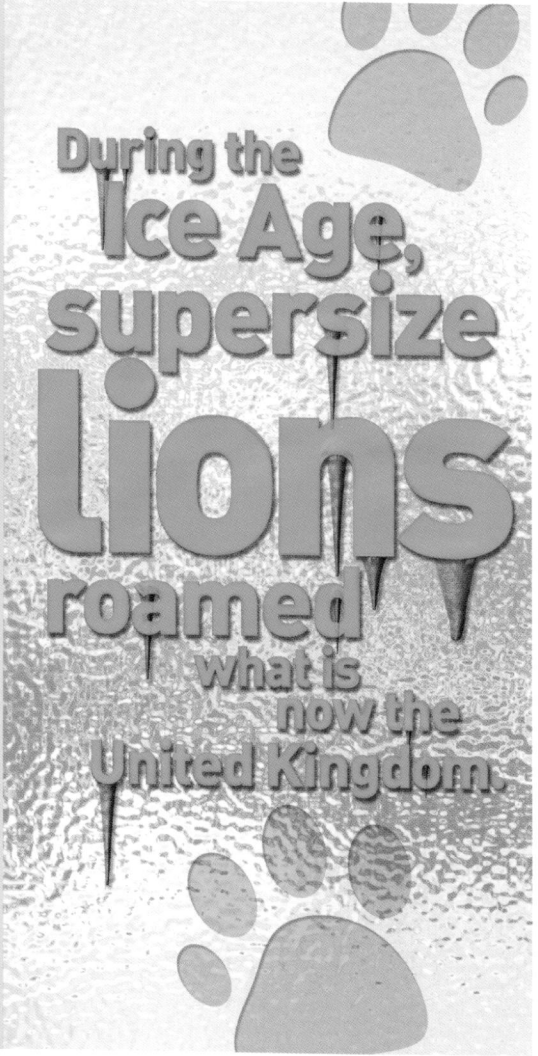
During the Ice Age, supersize lions roamed what is now the United Kingdom.

HUMMINGBIRDS
FLAP THEIR
WINGS UP TO
80 TIMES
A SECOND.

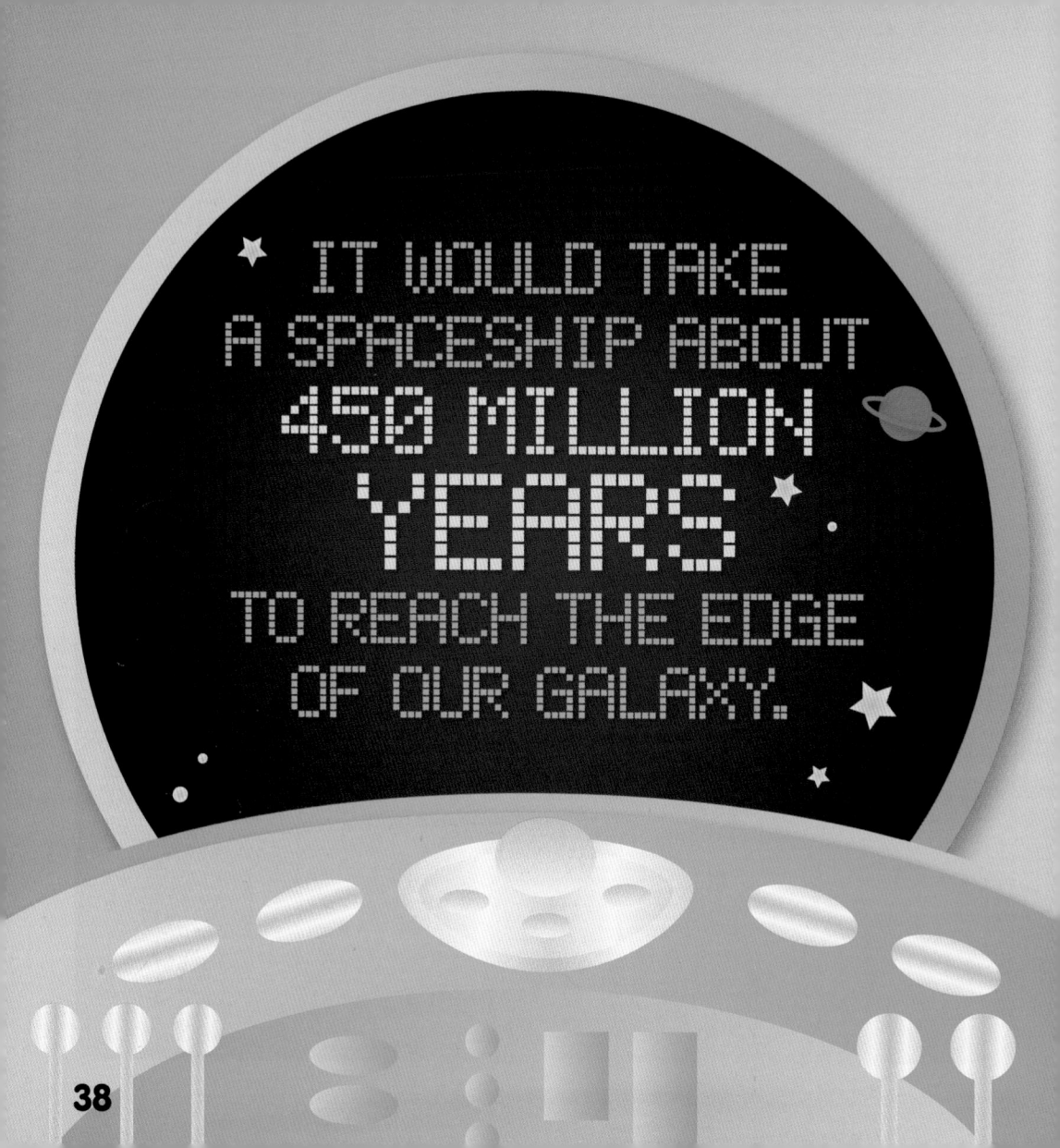
IT WOULD TAKE
A SPACESHIP ABOUT
450 MILLION
YEARS
TO REACH THE EDGE
OF OUR GALAXY.

A HIKER IN COLORADO, U.S.A., SCARED OFF A MOUNTAIN LION THAT WAS STALKING HER BY SINGING OPERA.

A KIND OF BIRD THAT LIVED 25 MILLION YEARS AGO HAD A WINGSPAN LONGER THAN SIX BASEBALL BATS.

SOME RAINBOWS APPEAR TO

CONTAIN ONLY SHADES OF RED.

About
400 hours
of new videos
are posted to
YouTube
every minute.

ONE WOMAN WALKED 10,000 MILES (16,093 km) ACROSS ASIA AND AUSTRALIA IN THREE YEARS.

SPUTNIK 1, THE FIRST SATELLITE IN SPACE, WAS ABOUT THE SIZE OF A BEACH BALL.

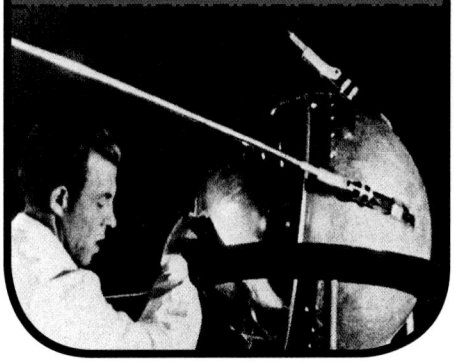

Hundreds of years ago, it was common for people in Naples, Italy, TO EAT PASTA WITH THEIR BARE HANDS.
The TIANJIN EYE, a Ferris wheel in CHINA, is suspended over the Hai River.
Some BIRDS eat BEESWAX.
In Spanish-speaking countries, the toxic manchineel tree is known as the "TREE OF DEATH."
Thousands of bacteria live on just one STRAND of your HAIR.
An unmanned AIR FORCE plane spent 718 DAYS ORBITING EARTH.
March 6 is NATIONAL OREO DAY in the United States.
A man in the United Kingdom TRAINED his cocker spaniel to RESCUE LOST CATS.
44

Deep-sea creatures called LARVACEANS create "HOUSES" OUT OF THEIR SNOT.

A chef in New York City created a savory doughnut made out of spaghetti.

The EXOPLANET KELT-11b is 40 PERCENT LARGER than JUPITER but is about as DENSE AS STYROFOAM.

THE WALNUT SPHINX CATERPILLAR makes a whistling sound TO SCARE OFF HUNGRY BIRDS.

A SHORTFIN MAKO SHARK traveled more than 11,600 miles (18,670 km) in one year—that's almost halfway around the world.

At an annual race in Totnes, England, competitors kick oranges along the course as they run.

On average, a $1 bill is in circulation in the United States for about six years.

The first item sold on eBay was a broken laser pointer.

A cobra bit a chef in China 20 minutes AFTER its head had been CUT from its body.

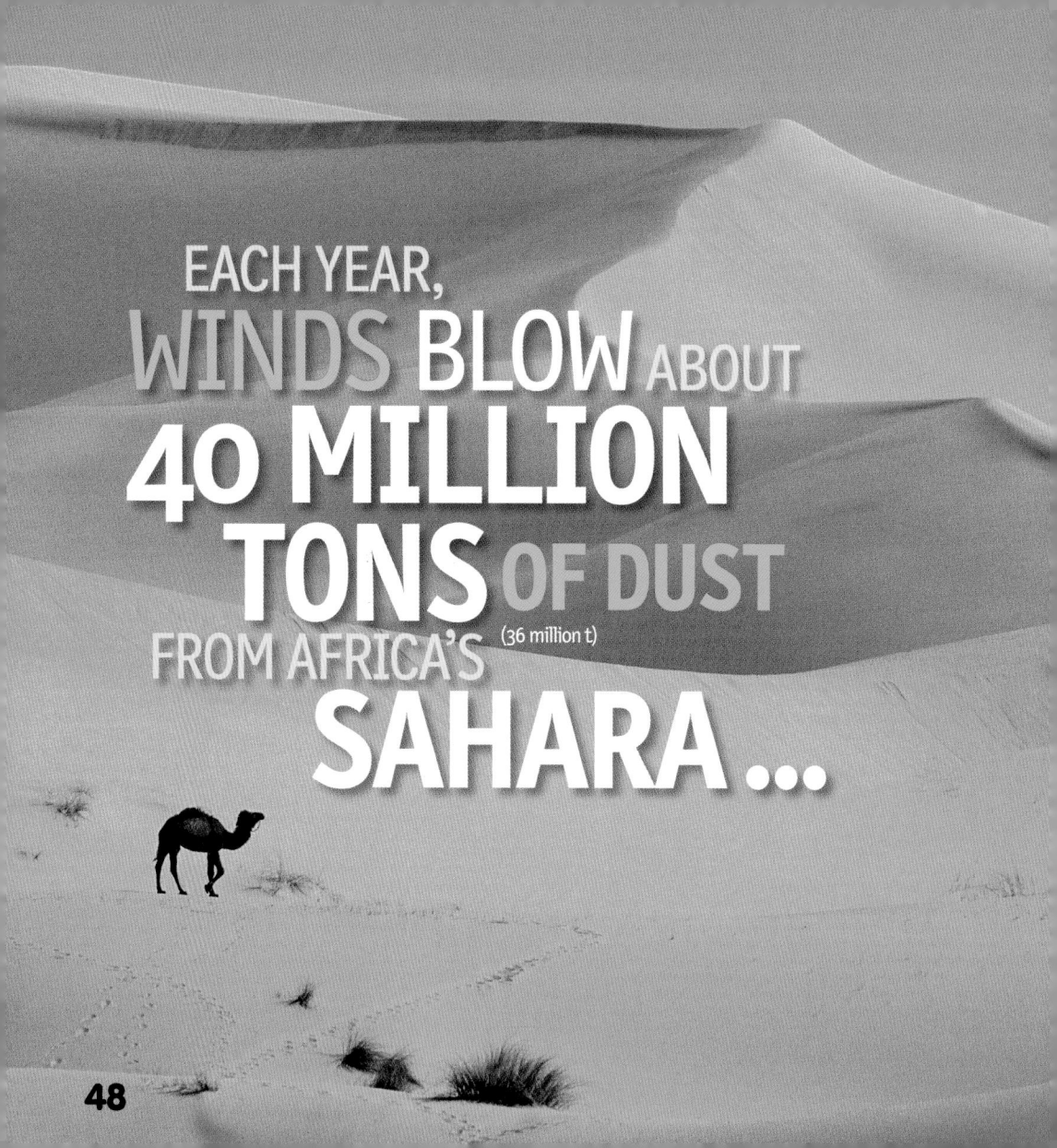
EACH YEAR,
WINDS BLOW ABOUT
40 MILLION
TONS OF DUST
(36 million t)
FROM AFRICA'S
SAHARA...

TO THE
AMAZON
RIVER BASIN
IN SOUTH AMERICA

There are
more than
20,000
TV stations
in the world.

FOUND IN AUSTRALIA AND NEW GUINEA, THE **SOUTHERN CASSOWARY BIRD** HAS CLAWS NEARLY THE LENGTH OF AN iPHONE.

The **coati,** a member of the raccoon family, can rotate its ankles **180 degrees.**

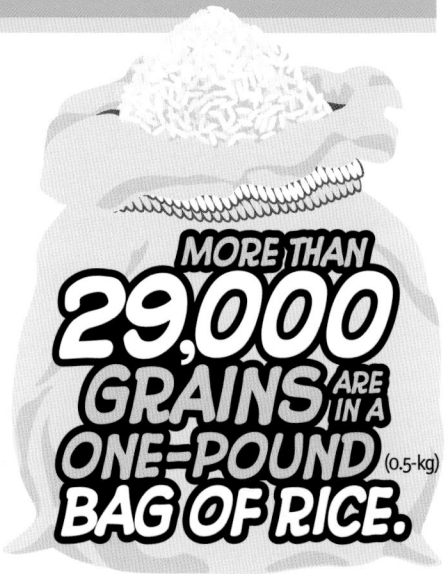

A
HEXAGON-
SHAPED
HURRICANE
HAS HOVERED
OVER SATURN'S
NORTH POLE
FOR AT LEAST
30 YEARS.

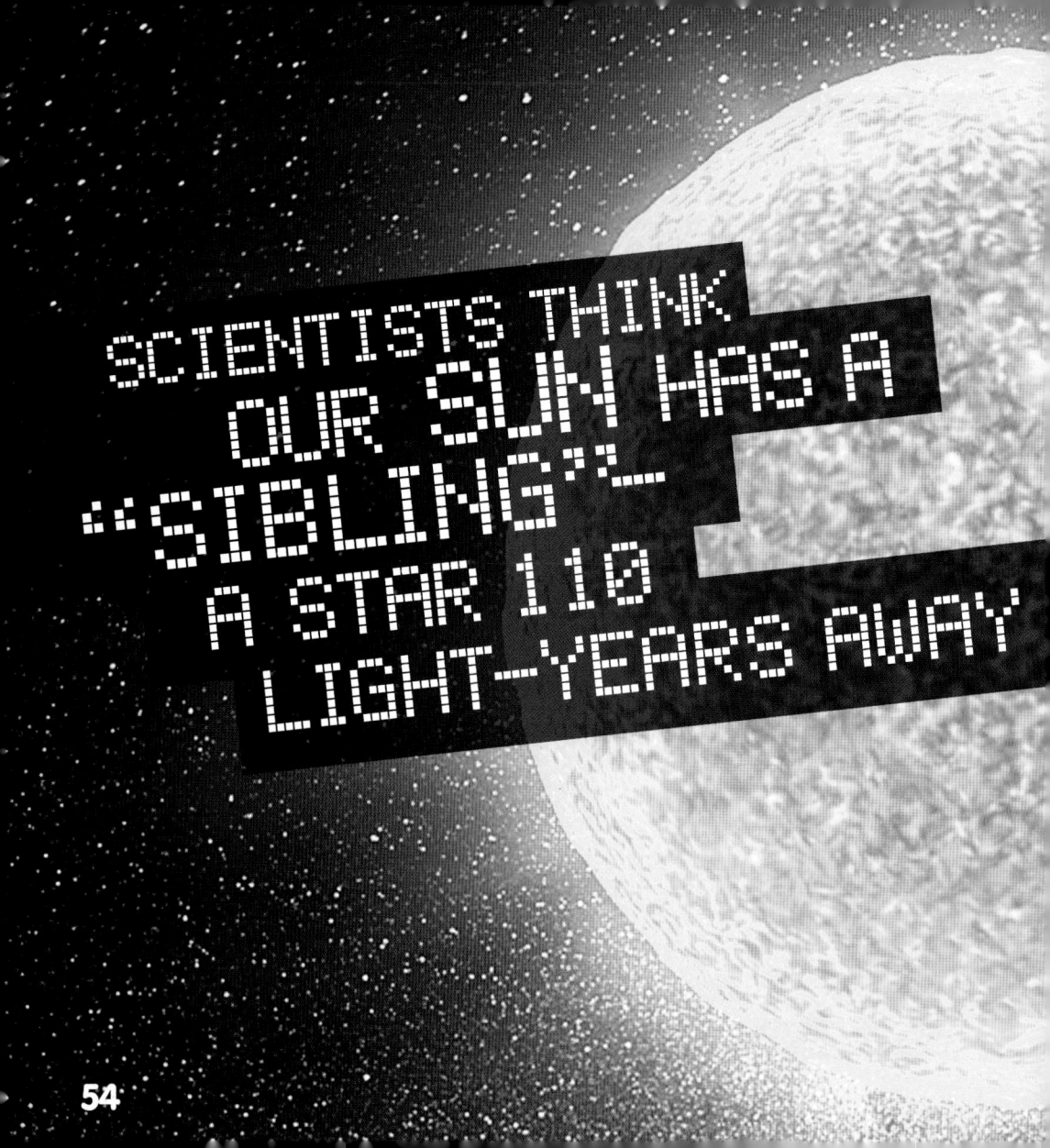
SCIENTISTS THINK
OUR SUN HAS A
"SIBLING"—
A STAR 110
LIGHT-YEARS AWAY

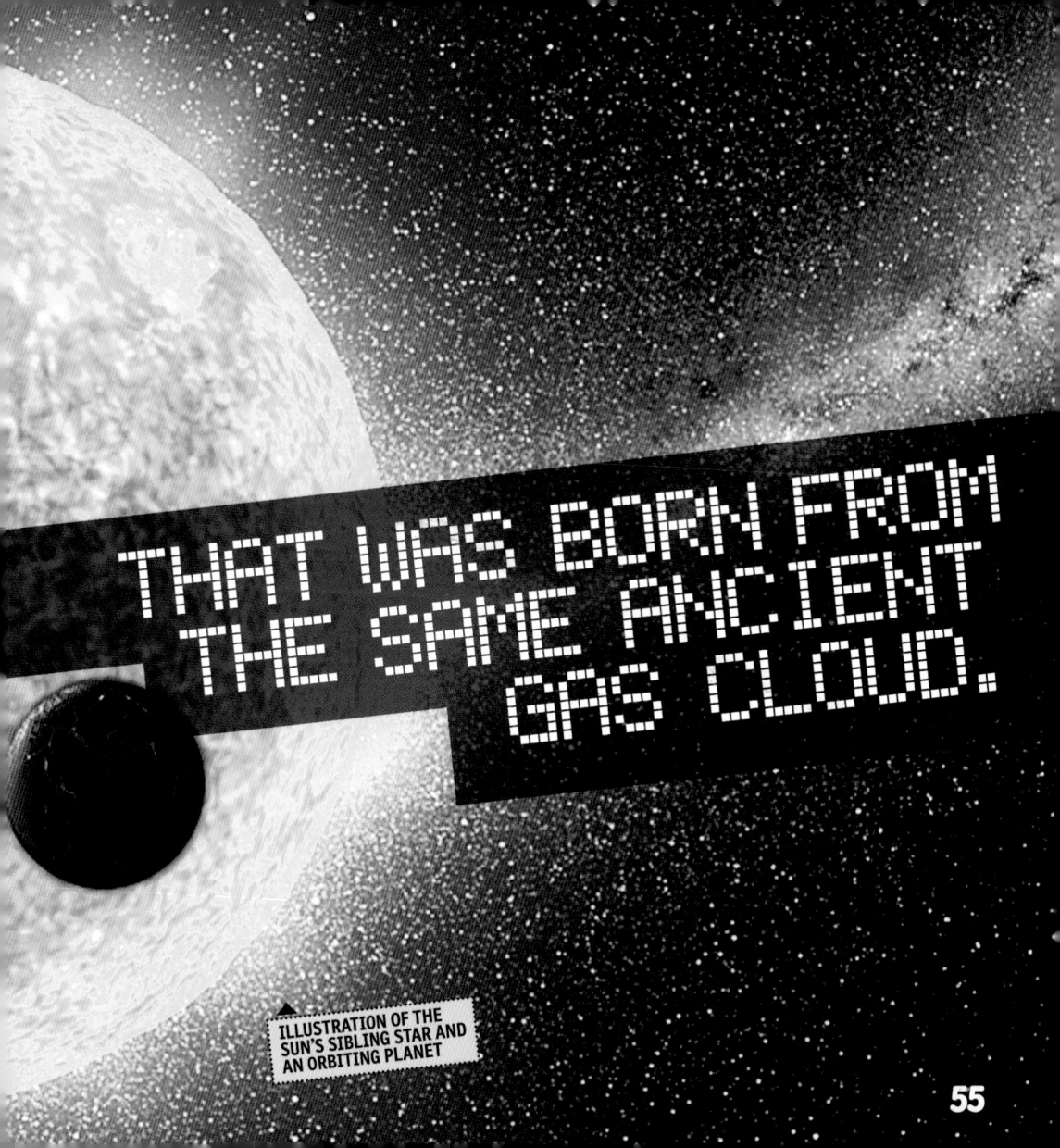

ILLUSTRATION OF THE SUN'S SIBLING STAR AND AN ORBITING PLANET

A group of
Twitter
users in Japan
once posted
143,199
tweets in
one second.

A STUDY FOUND THAT THE **LONGER YOU SLEEP,** THE STRANGER YOUR **DREAMS** BECOME.

VOLCANOES ONCE ERUPTED ON THE MOON.

Hello Kitty's full name is Kitty White.

LIFTING WEIGHTS
MAY IMPROVE
YOUR
MEMORY.

Tortoises can crawl about one mile an hour.
(1.6 km/h)
WAIT FOR ME, GUYS!

A FRESHWATER LAKE THE SIZE OF LAKE ONTARIO IS HIDDEN UNDER NEARLY 2.5 MILES OF ICE (4 km) IN ANTARCTICA.

More American cash is spent outside the United States than inside its borders.

At the Starbucks in CIA headquarters, in Virginia, U.S.A., workers aren't allowed to write customers' names on cups.

THESE PLANTS
CAN KILL

THE POISON GARDEN IN NORTH ENGLAND IS A PUBLIC GARDEN FILLED WITH DEADLY PLANTS.

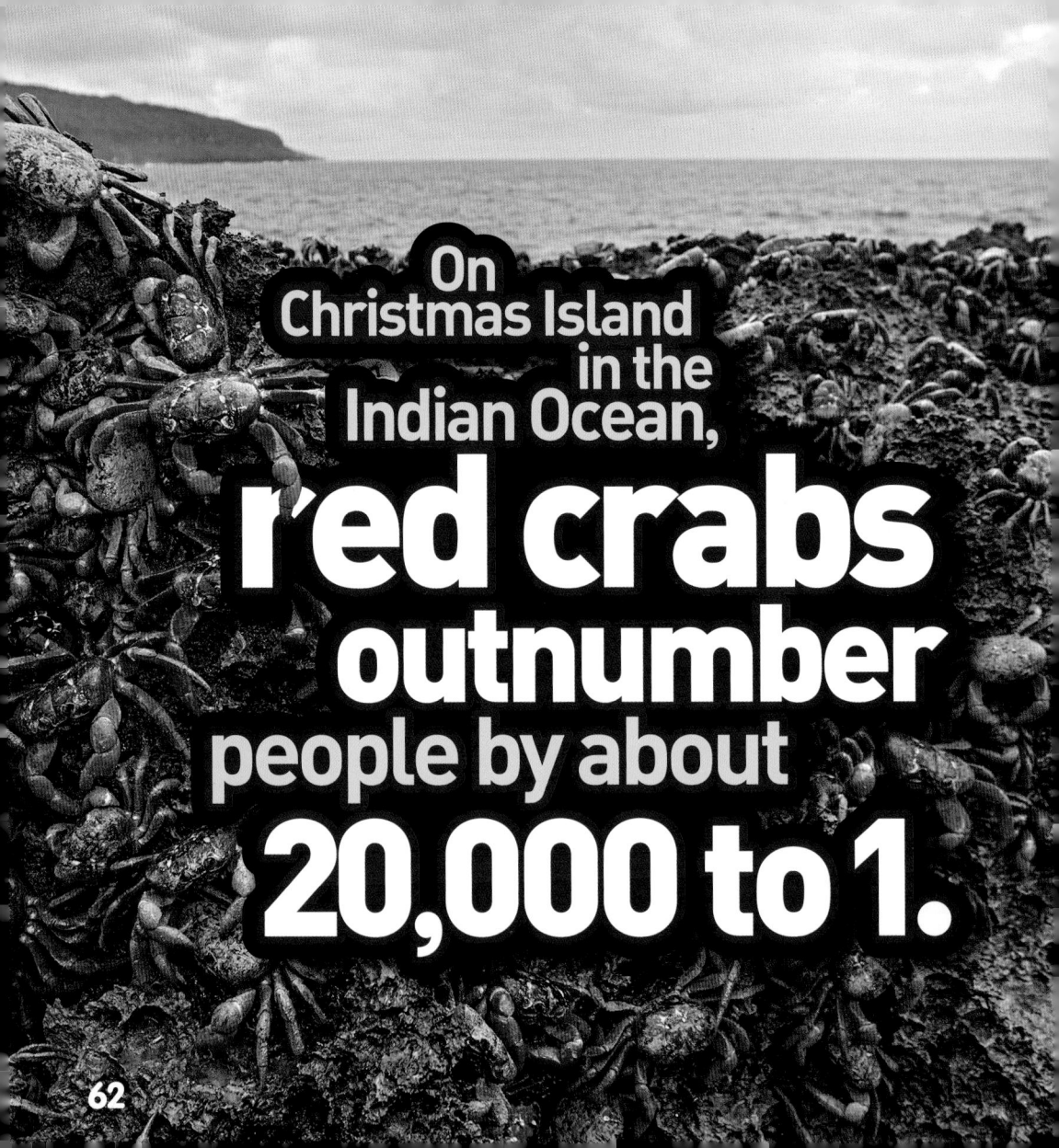

On Christmas Island in the Indian Ocean, **r'ed crabs outnumber** people by about **20,000 to 1.**

FLASHES OF LIGHT SOMETIMES APPEAR IN THE SKY BEFORE AND DURING EARTHQUAKES.

A WIND TURBINE IN DENMARK IS AS TALL AS A 72-STORY BUILDING.

THE ARCHES OF A McDONALD'S IN SEDONA, ARIZONA, U.S.A., ARE TURQUOISE INSTEAD OF YELLOW.

A CHOCOLATE BAR NAMED

CHICKEN DINNER

USED TO BE SOLD IN THE UNITED STATES.

Just a teaspoon (5 mL) of a neutron star's matter would weigh six billion tons. (5.5 billion t)

About 30 million American adults don't use the Internet—more people than the entire population of Nepal.

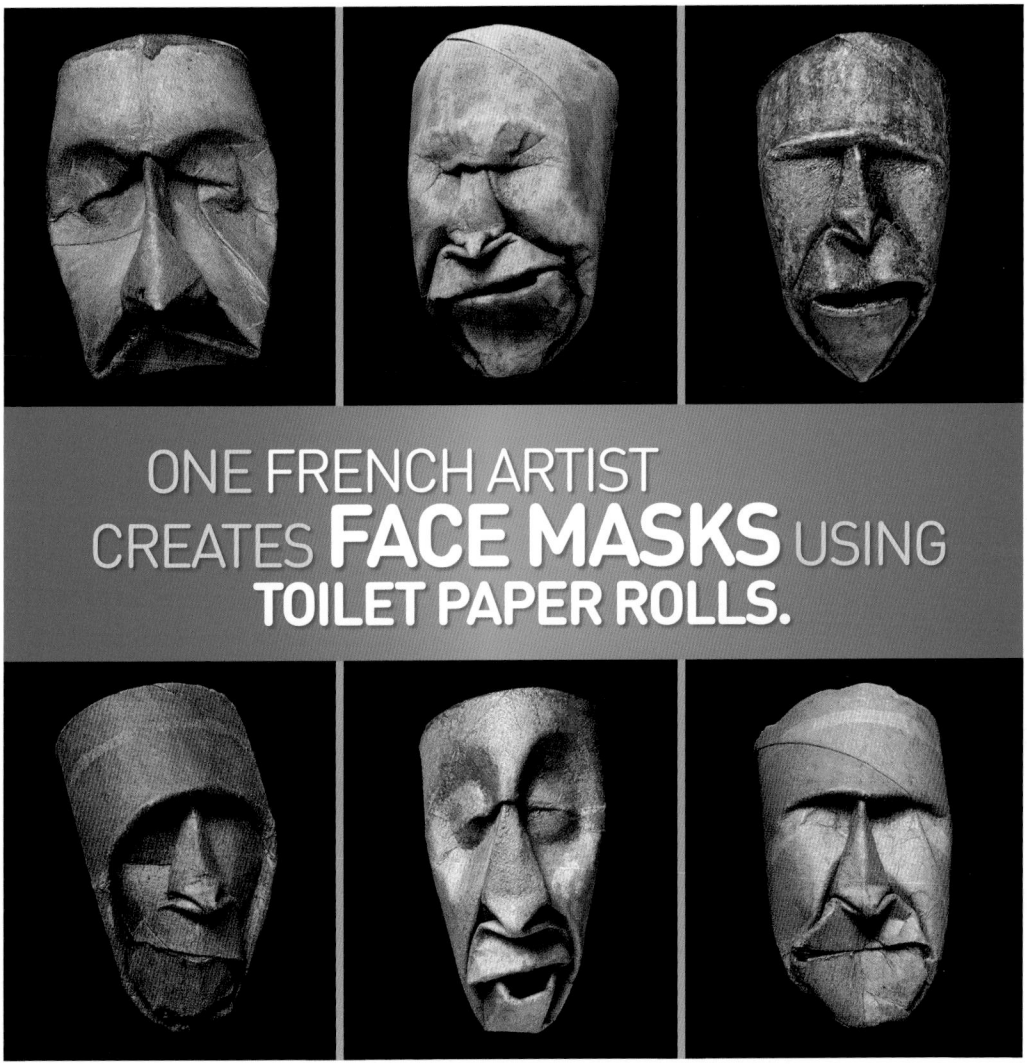
ONE FRENCH ARTIST
CREATES FACE MASKS USING
TOILET PAPER ROLLS.

A GROUP OF GOATS

IS CALLED A TRIP.

In Japan, you can buy doughnuts stuffed with ramen noodles.

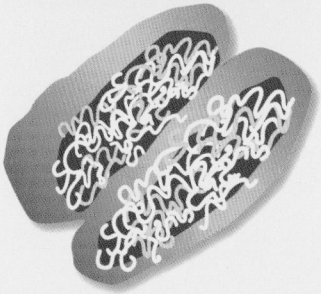

A **POMERANIAN** BECAME THE **FASTEST DOG** ON TWO PAWS AFTER WALKING NEARLY **33 FEET** (10 m) IN LESS THAN SEVEN SECONDS ON HIS **HIND LEGS.**

THE U.S.
SUPREME COURT
BUILDING IN WASHINGTON, D.C.,
HAS A BASKETBALL
COURT ON ITS TOP FLOOR.

NEW YORK CITY'S
NEW YEAR'S EVE
BALL IS MADE UP OF
2,688
CRYSTAL PANELS.

A STUDY FOUND THAT
BABIES BORN IN WINTER
TEND TO CRAWL SOONER THAN
BABIES BORN IN SUMMER.

A Dutch artist created a 69-foot-long (21-m) wooden hippo and floated it down London's River Thames.

A FARMER IN CHINA GROWS
PEARS SHAPED LIKE BABIES.

Restaurant **diners** who sit by a window tend to order **salads** more often, according to one study.

Osprey birds build nests **big enough** to fit an **adult human inside.**

Walt Disney World's *Cinderella* **Castle** contains a *hotel suite* that **sleeps** six people.

A company in the Middle East makes bodysuits for camels

to wear while training for races.

THE
AMAZON
RAIN FOREST
IS ABOUT TWICE
THE SIZE OF
INDIA.
MORE THAN
100 MILLION
YEARS AGO,
INDIA WAS AN
ISLAND.

Male walruses make a bell-like sound to attract mates.

A MAN
IN ILLINOIS, U.S.A.,
BUILT A PICKUP
TRUCK
THAT LOOKS
AS IF IT HAS BEEN
FLIPPED
UPSIDE DOWN.

Hagfish digest food through their skin.

Mexico once had three different presidents in power in one day.
An Indian man set a world record by drumming 2,109 drumbeats in one minute.
ALBERT EINSTEIN'S EYEBALLS ARE KEPT IN A SAFE-DEPOSIT BOX IN NEW YORK CITY.
loudest
bicycle
horn
is louder
than an

A BEAVER'S IRON-RICH DIET TURNS ITS FRONT TEETH ORANGE.

There are more than 1,000 varieties of mango.

IN 12TH-CENTURY CHINA, PEOPLE WORE SUNGLASSES WITH LENSES MADE FROM QUARTZ, A TYPE OF CRYSTAL.

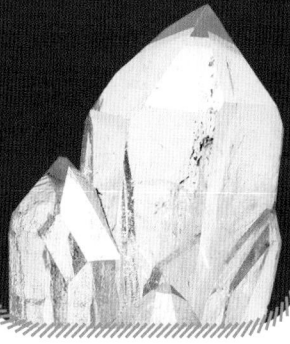

The biggest x-ray laser in the world CAN PRODUCE 27,000 LIGHT FLASHES in one second.

THE REAL-LIFE GLACIER FEATURED IN *STAR WARS: EPISODE V THE EMPIRE STRIKES BACK* AS PLANET **HOTH** COULD DISAPPEAR ENTIRELY BY 2100.

THE ATLANTIC OCEAN GROWS WIDER BY ABOUT AN INCH (2.5 CM) EVERY YEAR.

The **BRAINS** of some **SPIDERS** GROW into their **LEGS.**

Some **200 GALLONS** (757 L) of **CREAM** SPILLED INTO A SEWER in Richmond, Virginia, U.S.A.

THIEVES IN ENGLAND STOLE 24,000 BEES FROM A COUNTRY ESTATE.

DINERS at a restaurant in TORONTO, CANADA, eat completely in THE DARK.

DINERS are more likely to order an item if **IT IS LISTED INSIDE A BOX** on the **MENU.**

STUDENTS in ancient Greece wore necklaces of **ROSEMARY** to help them **WITH THEIR EXAMS.**

A SOLAR-ENERGY FARM in Morocco is the size of about **260 FOOTBALL FIELDS.**

The town of **BORING, OREGON, U.S.A.,** is a sister city of the town of **DULL, SCOTLAND.**

The **TERM "ASTRONAUT"** comes from **GREEK** words meaning **"STAR SAILOR."**

Australia's
Great Barrier
Reef
is roughly the size
of Italy.

A **crosswalk light** in Lisbon, Portugal, featured a figure **dancing to music** as the **stop signal.**

SOME **POLICE CARS** IN DUBAI, UNITED ARAB EMIRATES, CAN GO MORE THAN **220 MILES** (354 km/h) AN HOUR.

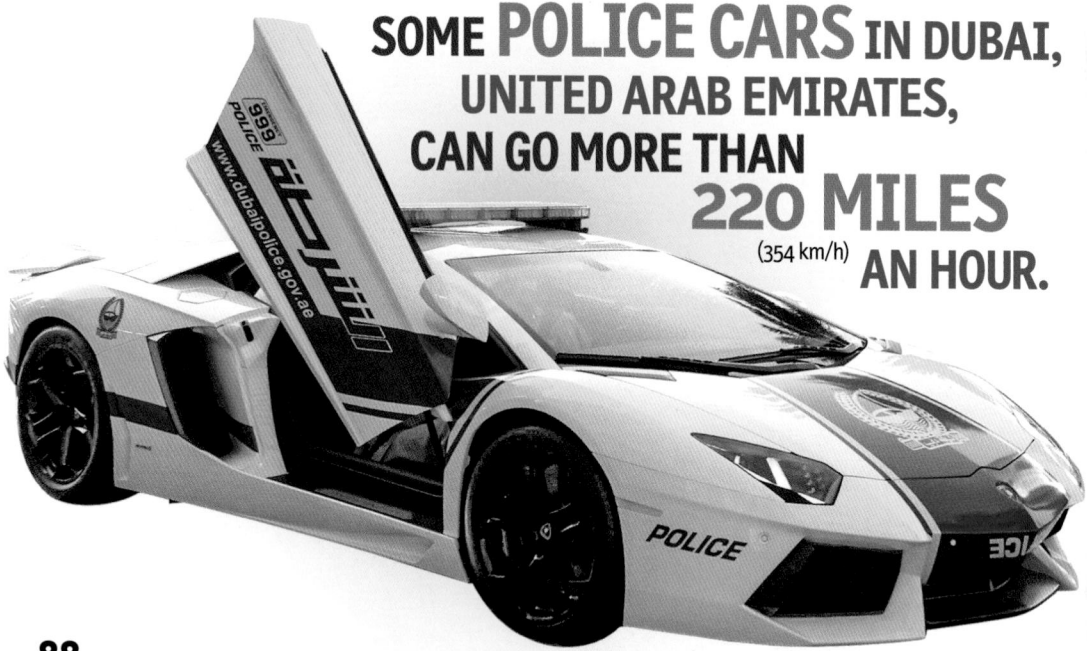

THERE ARE
FIVE TIMES
AS MANY
BICYCLES
AS CARS IN
COPENHAGEN,
DENMARK.

IT'S IMPOSSIBLE
FOR A BAT TO STAND
UPRIGHT.

TOGETHER, A
TARSIER'S
EYES
WEIGH NEARLY AS
MUCH AS
ITS BRAIN.
As a training tool, the U.S. military
created a plan to
combat zombies.

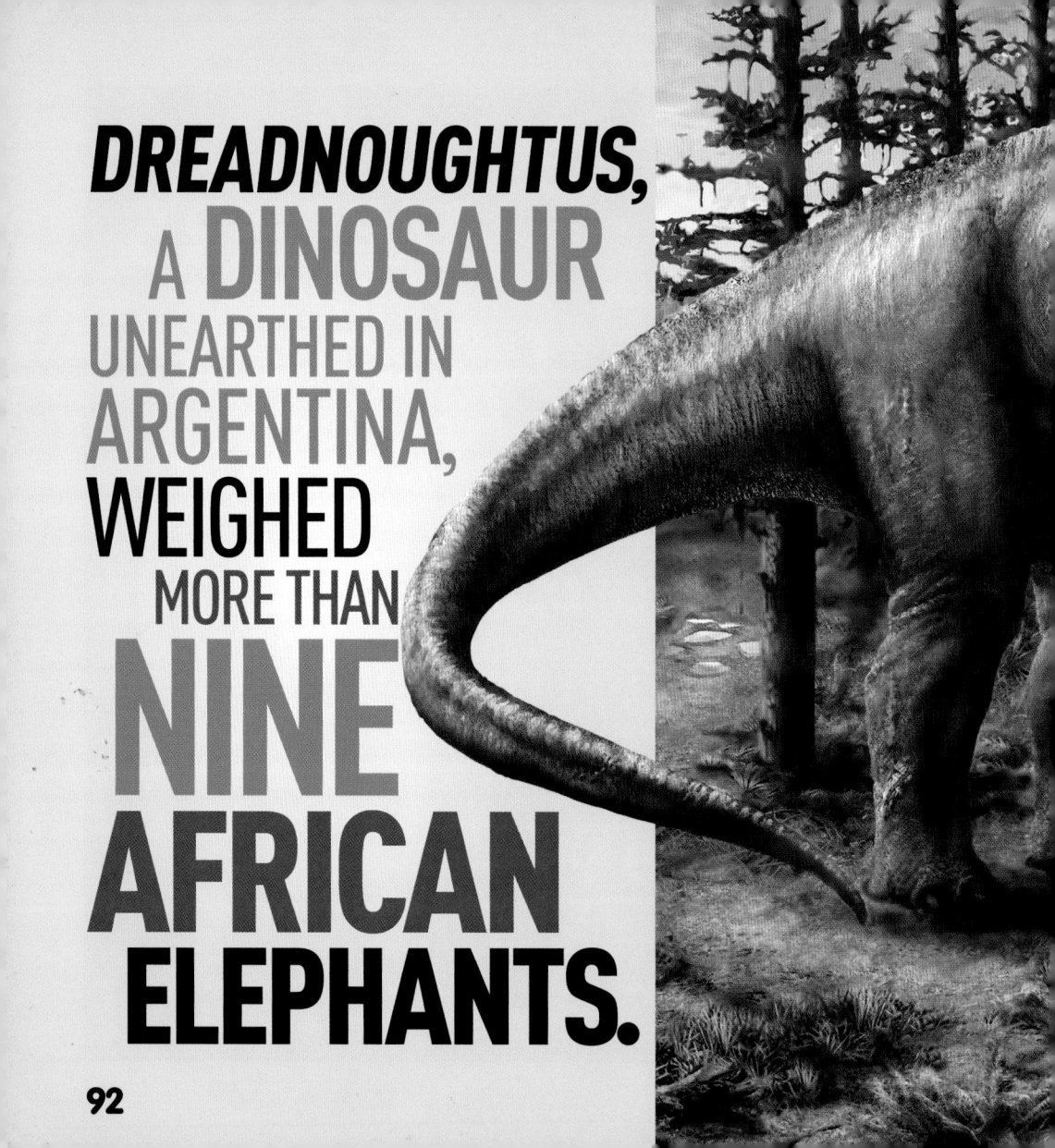

DREADNOUGHTUS, A **DINOSAUR** UNEARTHED IN ARGENTINA, WEIGHED MORE THAN **NINE AFRICAN ELEPHANTS.**

By snapping its claw, the pistol shrimp creates a jet of water that can travel 62 miles (100 km/h) an hour.

Roman gladiators consumed an energy drink containing ash.

Algae sometimes grow on sloth fur.

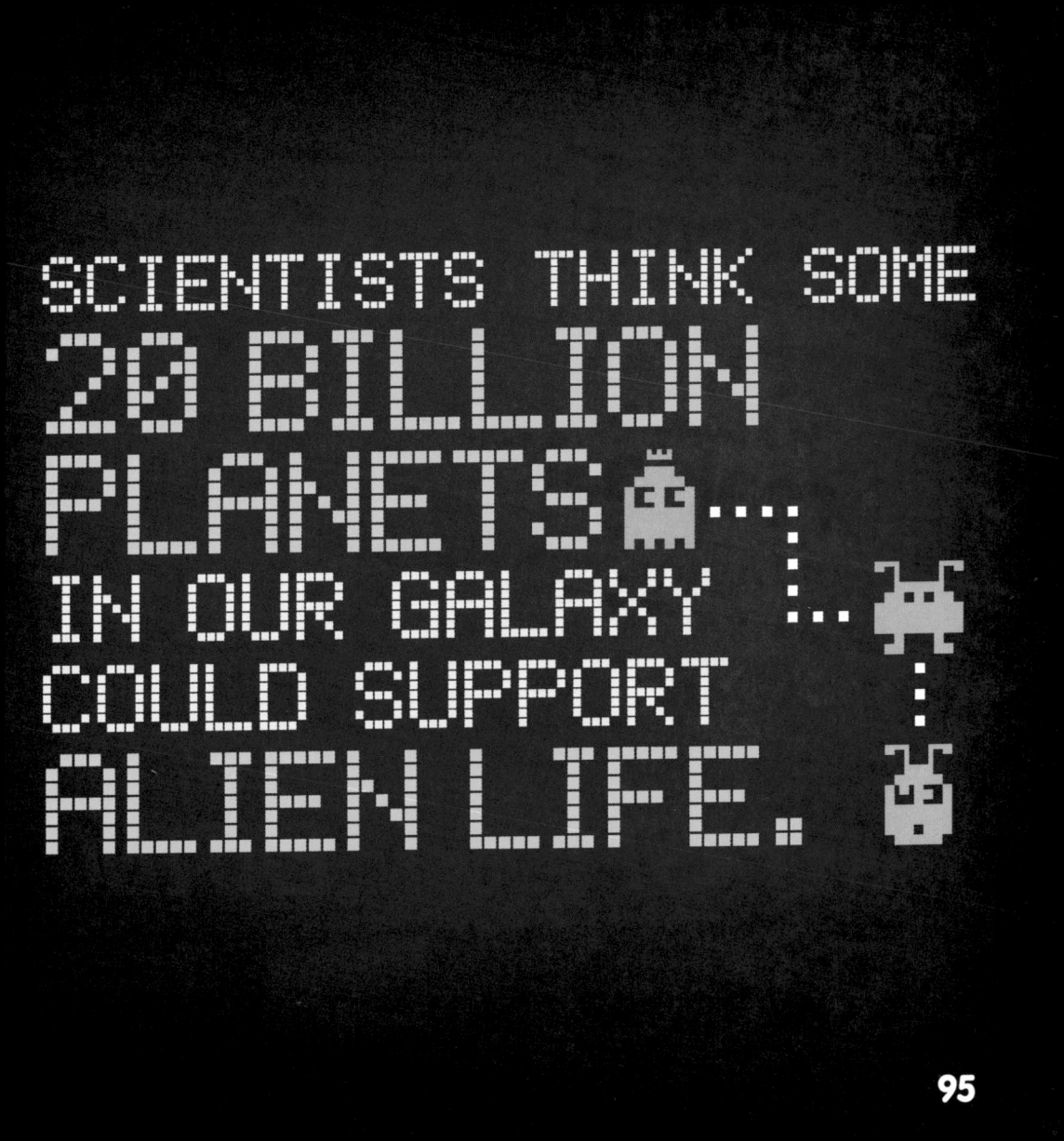
SCIENTISTS THINK SOME
20 BILLION
PLANETS
IN OUR GALAXY
COULD SUPPORT
ALIEN LIFE.

AN OREGON MAN MADE A 40-FOOT-TALL (12-m) NUTCRACKER THAT CAN CRACK COCONUTS.

SCIENTISTS CREATED A **FORK** THAT MEASURES HOW LONG YOU PAUSE BETWEEN BITES TO SHOW ***HOW FAST YOU'RE EATING.***

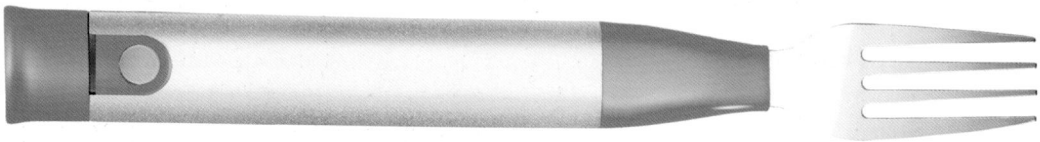

SOME KINDS OF **APPLES** ARE **PINK** ON THE INSIDE.

The first steam **locomotive** made in the United States lost a race to a **horse.**

SOME OLD JETS ARE PLACED

IN AIRPLANE GRAVEYARDS.

CAMELS ARE BORN WITHOUT HUMPS.

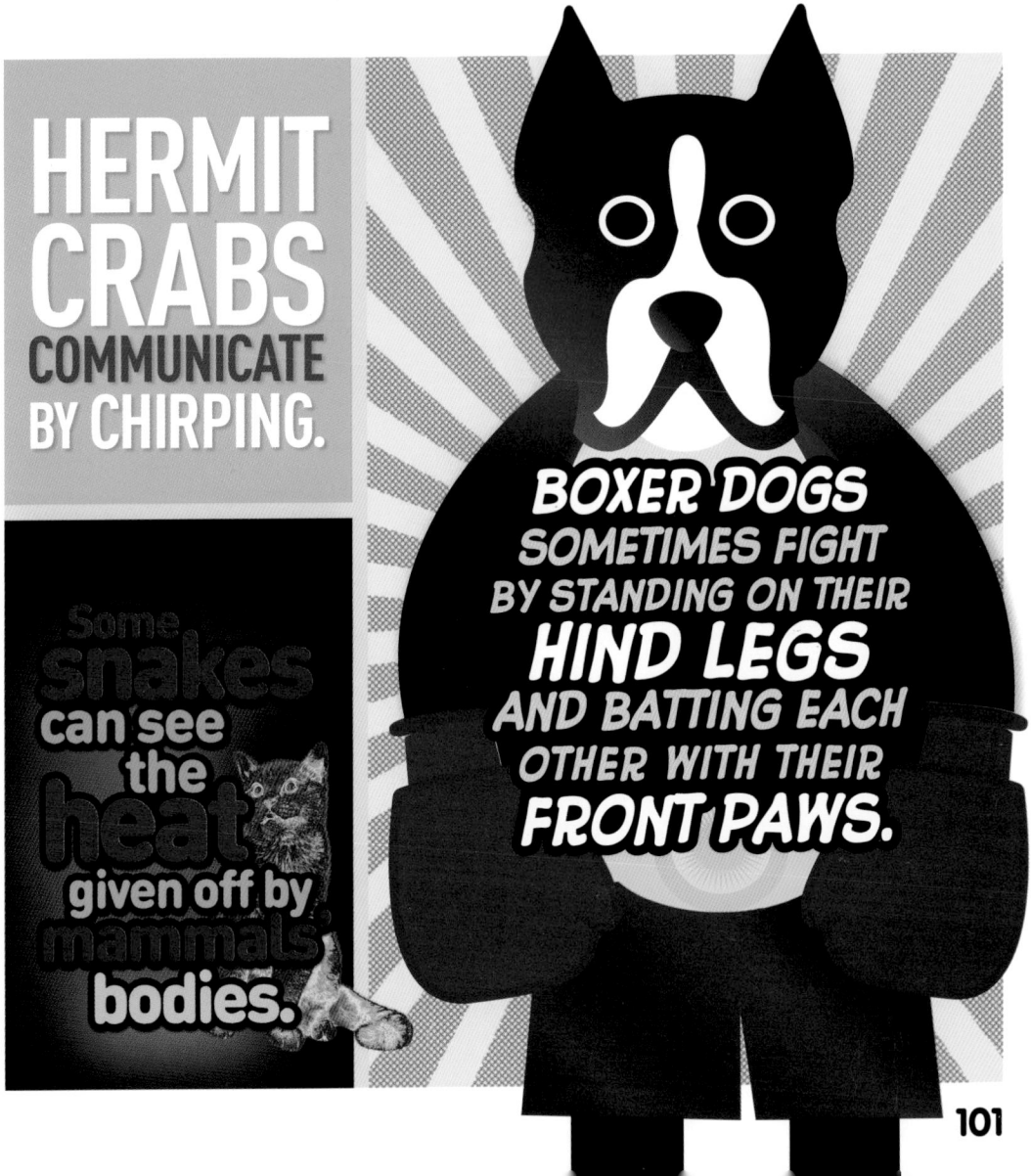
HERMIT CRABS COMMUNICATE BY CHIRPING.
Some snakes can see the heat given off by mammals' bodies.
BOXER DOGS SOMETIMES FIGHT BY STANDING ON THEIR HIND LEGS AND BATTING EACH OTHER WITH THEIR FRONT PAWS.

Some worms that live on coral reefs look like tiny, colorful Christmas trees.

Scientists used a robot disguised as a penguin to study real emperor penguins.

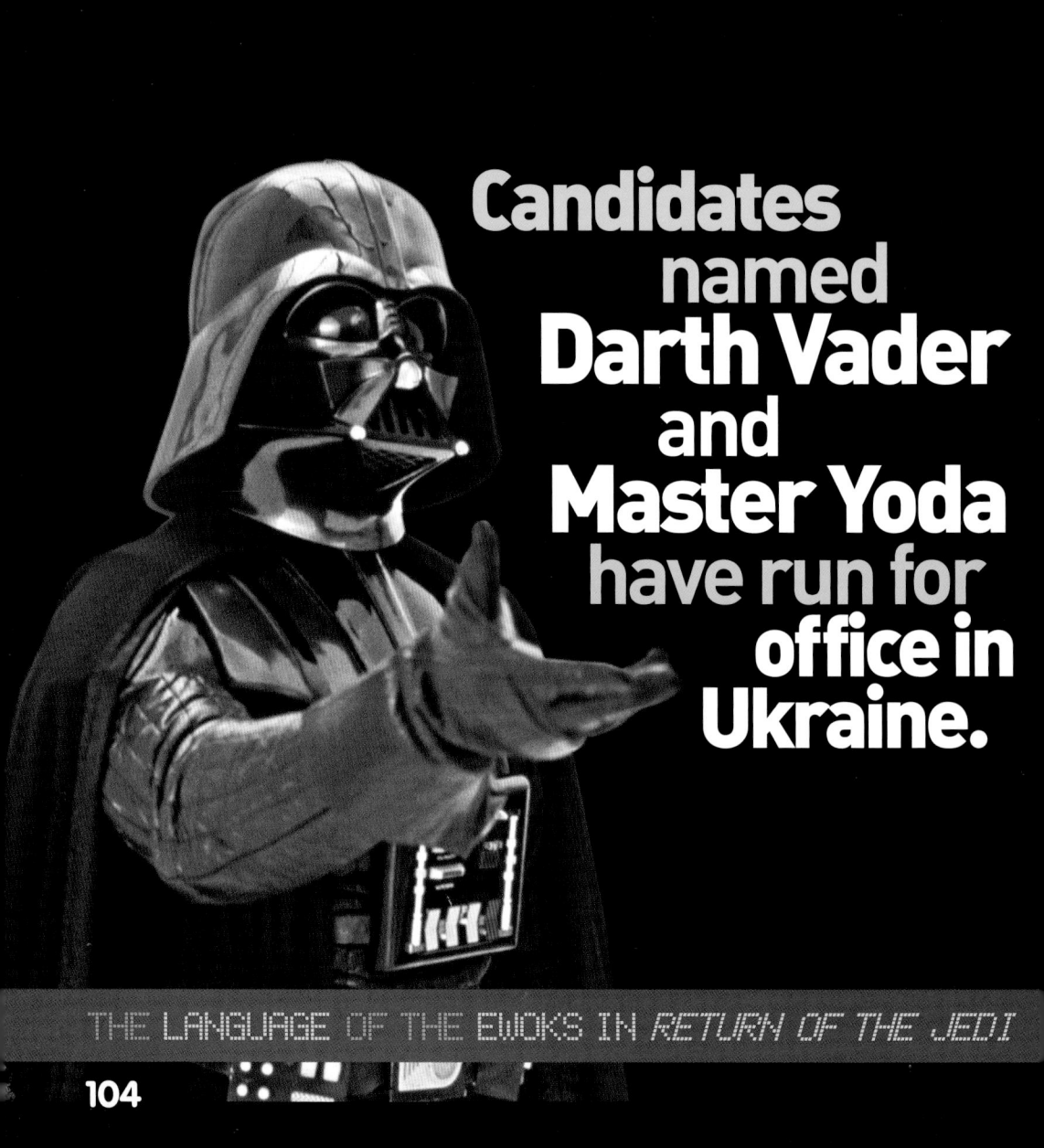

THE LANGUAGE OF THE EWOKS IN *RETURN OF THE JEDI*

A MAN BUILT **A DRONE** THAT LOOKS LIKE HAN SOLO'S SHIP, THE ***MILLENNIUM FALCON.***

IS PARTLY BASED ON TIBETAN AND NEPALI.

IN 1921,

NEARLY

76

(193 cm) INCHES

OF SNOW

FELL IN

24 HOURS

ON SILVER LAKE,

COLORADO, U.S.A.

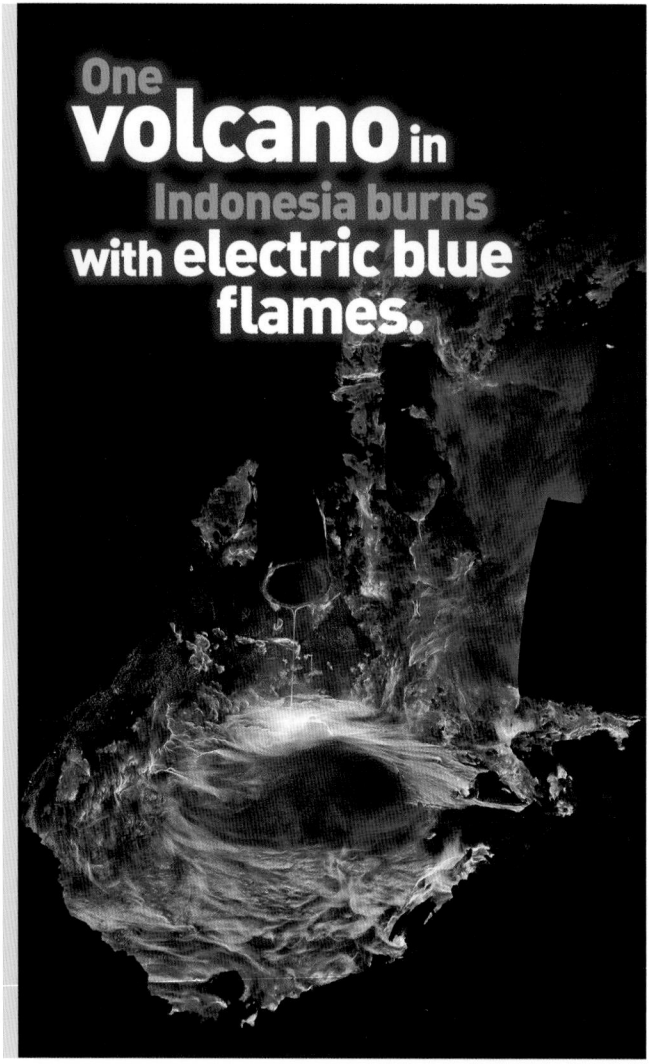

The Super Soaker water gun was originally called the Power Drencher.

EVERY DAY, 100 TONS OF (91 t) COSMIC DUST FROM SPACE ENTERS EARTH'S ATMOSPHERE—THAT'S THE SAME WEIGHT AS 400 MOUNTAIN GORILLAS.

HERDS OF BUFFALO-SIZE RODENTS ONCE ROAMED SOUTH AMERICA.

HONEYPOT WORKER **ANTS,** WHICH STORE **NECTAR IN THEIR BODIES,** CAN SWELL TO THE SIZE OF A **GRAPE.**

Shoppers are more likely to buy a product if they touch it, one study found.

THE TEETH OF AT LEAST TWO SHARK SPECIES ARE NATURALLY COATED IN FLUORIDE, A MAIN INGREDIENT IN TOOTHPASTE.

IN SAGADA, PHILIPPINES, **COFFINS** ARE ***NAILED*** TO A CLIFF FACE RATHER THAN **BURIED** UNDERGROUND.

CUCUMBERS WERE KNOWN AS "COWCUMBERS" UNTIL THE MID-19TH CENTURY.

LOUISIANA, U.S.A.,
IS HOME TO SOME
500,000
WILD PIGS.

A New York City artist invented a waffle iron that makes waffles shaped like a computer keyboard.

COFFEE WITH CREAM STAYS HOTTER LONGER THAN PLAIN BLACK COFFEE.

AS A HEN GETS OLDER, SHE PRODUCES BIGGER EGGS.

THE INTERNATIONAL SPACE STATION WEIGHS MORE THAN 300 CARS.

A WARM GOLF BALL WILL TRAVEL FARTHER THROUGH THE AIR THAN A COLD ONE.

Every year, 300 million golf balls are lost or thrown away in the United States.
GOLF WAS BANNED IN 15TH-CENTURY SCOTLAND.

ONE KIND OF MITE CAN
SPRINT
20 TIMES
FASTER
THAN A CHEETAH,
AS MEASURED IN BODY LENGTHS
TRAVELED EACH SECOND.

You can buy "**smartshoes**" that give directions by **buzzing** your left or right foot to **signal** which way to turn.

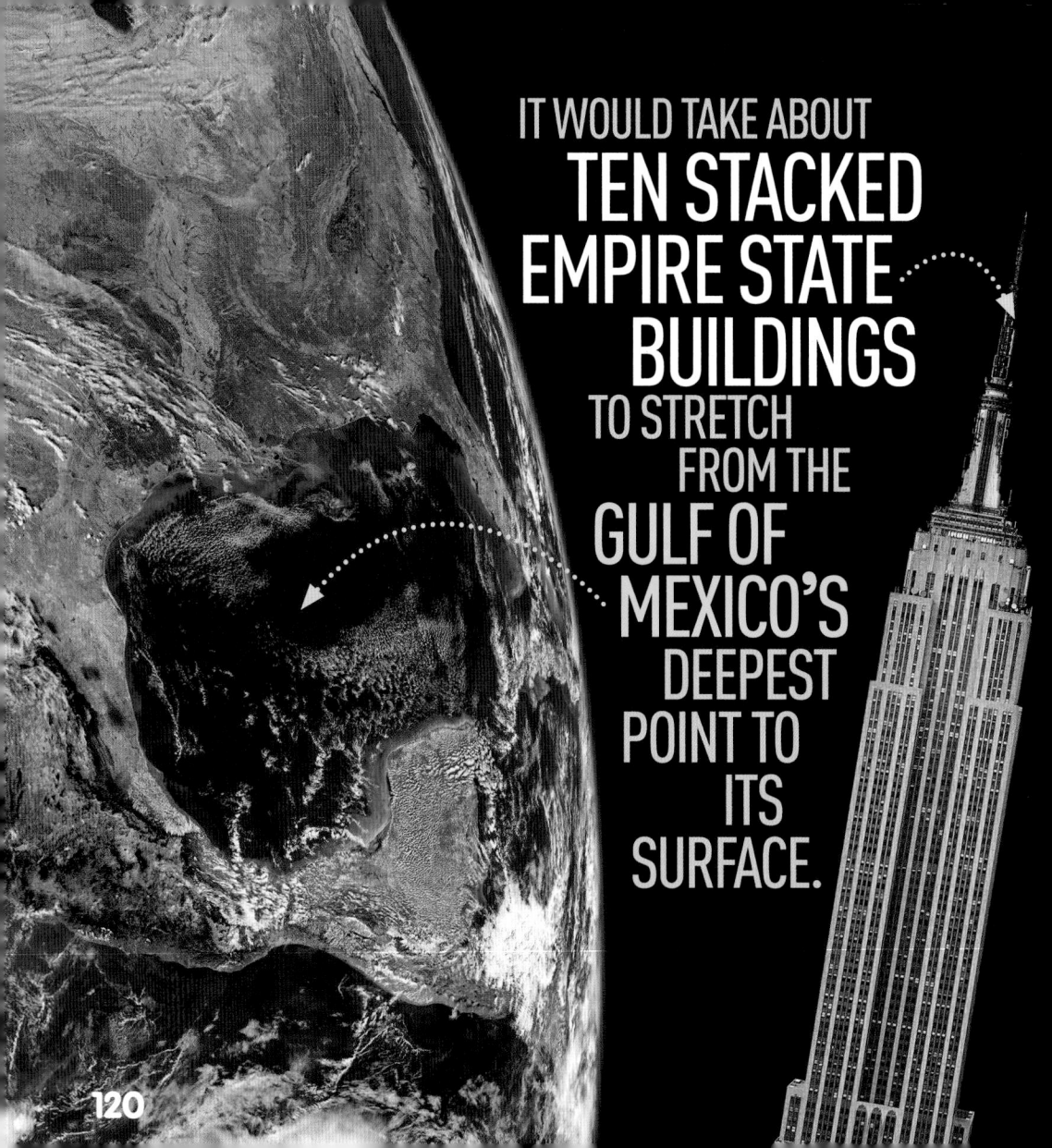

IT WOULD TAKE ABOUT **TEN STACKED EMPIRE STATE BUILDINGS** TO STRETCH FROM THE **GULF OF MEXICO'S** DEEPEST POINT TO ITS SURFACE.

Crocodiles sometimes climb trees.

WOOF!

ONE TYPE OF **OWL** IN AUSTRALIA **BARKS** LIKE A **DOG.**

DUST STORMS ON MARS CAN GROW BIGGER THAN THE CONTINENTAL UNITED STATES.

One fast-food chain INVENTED THE FRORK—a fork to eat FRENCH FRIES.

A TEENAGER'S BURIED TREASURE from 1981 was recently DISCOVERED in a VILLAGE in ENGLAND.

More than one million volcanoes are UNDER EARTH'S OCEAN.

VISITORS to a park in SINGAPORE can sit under trees WHOSE "LEAVES" ARE MADE OF UMBRELLAS.

THE MOON TAKES THE SAME NUMBER OF DAYS TO ROTATE AROUND EARTH AS IT DOES TO SPIN ONCE ON ITS AXIS.

To help prevent drowning, inventors have created a NECKLACE that will INFLATE if you stay underwater too long.

DOLPHINS shed their OUTER LAYER of skin every TWO HOURS.

VOG = **TOXIC FOG CREATED BY VOLCANIC ERUPTIONS**

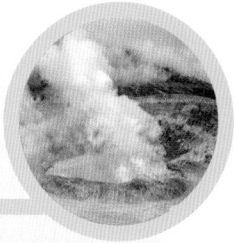

A COMPANY ONCE MADE **GUMBALLS** THAT LOOKED LIKE **MEATBALLS.**

A man in France recently discovered he was the **OWNER** of a **"LOST" DRAWING** by **Leonardo da Vinci** valued at **$15.8 MILLION.**

There is **STAR DUST** on city rooftops, sidewalks, and park benches.

IN CHURCHILL, CANADA, there is a **JAIL** for **POLAR BEARS.**

ICE SCULPTORS IN TEXAS, U.S.A., RE-CREATED SCENES FROM *FROSTY THE SNOWMAN* USING TWO MILLION POUNDS OF ICE.

Grasshopper Glacier in Montana, U.S.A., contains layers of grasshoppers preserved in ice.

Certain radio signals coming from Jupiter sound like popcorn popping.

1904
OVER 40 PERCENT OF AMERICANS
HAVE ANCESTORS WHO FIRST ENTERED THE UNITED STATES
THROUGH ELLIS ISLAND IN NEW YORK BAY.
CURIOUS GEORGE WAS ORIGINALLY NAMED FIFI.
SCIENTISTS LANDED A REMOTE-CONTROLLED SPACECRAFT ON A COMET THAT WAS TRAVELING 84,000 MILES (135,185 km/h) AN HOUR.

The cruise ship Queen Mary 2 has a plant that makes freshwater from saltwater.

The average car has some 25,000 parts.

THE CREATOR OF WONDER WOMAN ALSO INVENTED AN EARLY VERSION OF THE LIE DETECTOR.

IT TOOK THE INVENTOR OF THE RUBIK'S CUBE MORE THAN A MONTH TO SOLVE THE PUZZLE AFTER SCRAMBLING IT FOR THE FIRST TIME.

THE RUBIK'S CUBE WITH THE MOST SQUARES IS 17-BY-17-BY-17 CUBES.

Some streets in Seattle, Washington, U.S.A., boast artwork that only becomes visible when splashed with water.
11
9
10
7
8
6
5
4
2
3
1

The DISCO CLAM uses flashes of light reflected from its lips to ward off predators.

No cars are allowed on Sark Island in the English Channel.

THE AVERAGE PENCIL HAS ENOUGH GRAPHITE

AFRICA'S NILE RIVER IS LONGER THAN THE

TO DRAW A LINE THAT'S 35 MILES LONG.

(56 km)

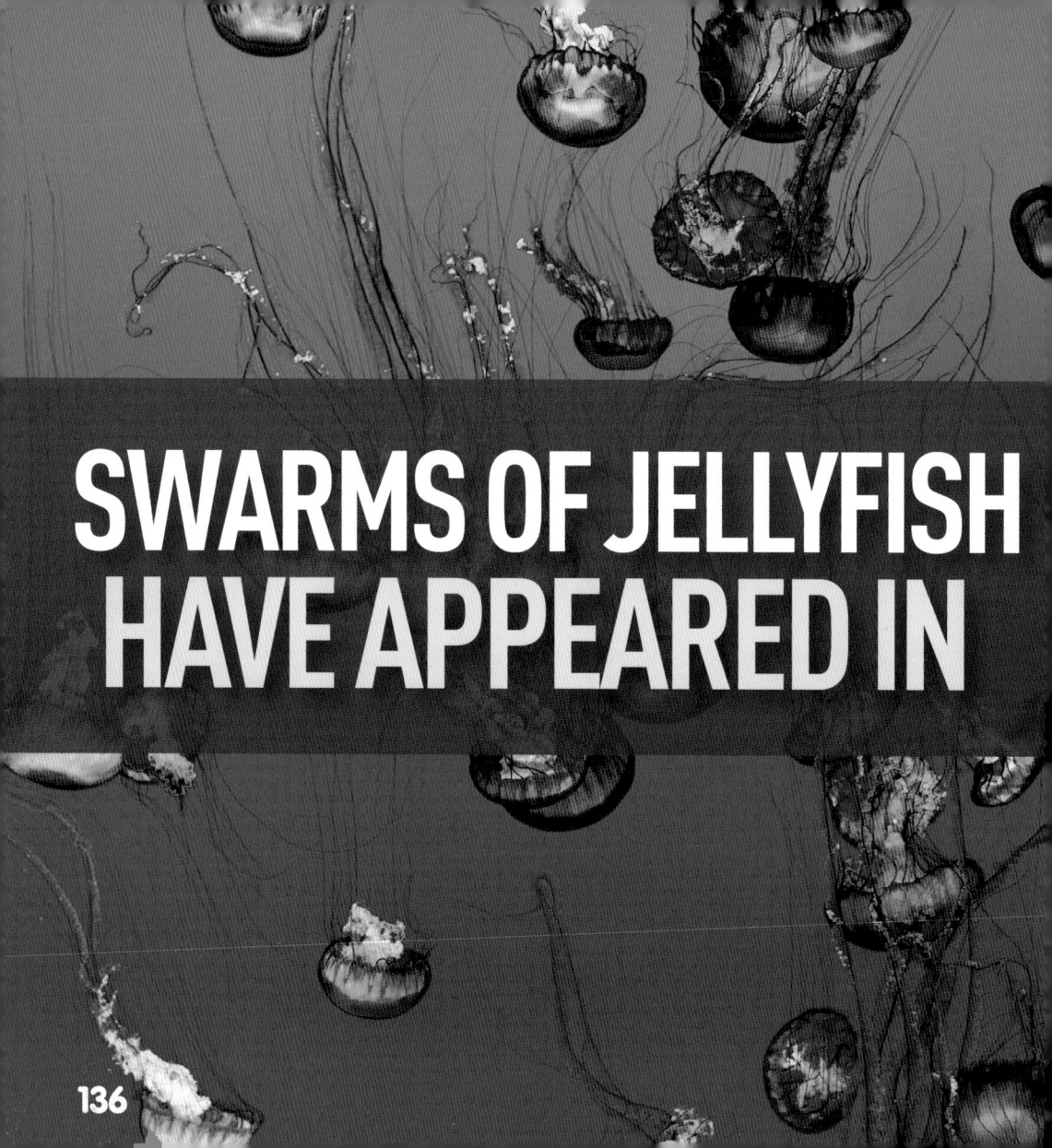

SWARMS OF JELLYFISH HAVE APPEARED IN

(161 km)

STRETCHING 100 MILES THE GULF OF MEXICO.

THE **DIVING BELL SPIDER** IS THE ONLY SPIDER THAT LIVES ITS **LIFE** ENTIRELY **UNDERWATER.**

THE PLANET KEPLER-413B WOBBLES LIKE A SPINNING TOP.

A study found that saying "**OW**" can help you tolerate pain better.

SEVERAL **CAVES** IN KENTUCKY, U.S.A., ARE HOME TO A SPECIES OF SEE-THROUGH, **EYELESS SHRIMP.**

NASA'S HUBBLE TELESCOPE CAPTURED AN IMAGE OF A GALAXY CLUSTER THAT LOOKS LIKE A SMILEY FACE.

THE POLICE SQUAD OF ONE SOUTHERN RUSSIAN TOWN WAS MADE UP ENTIRELY OF IDENTICAL TWINS.

You can cycle down a glow-in-the-dark bike path in the Netherlands.

MORE THAN 100 MILES (161 km) OF MINING TUNNELS EXIST UNDER DETROIT, MICHIGAN, U.S.A.

ONE ACRE (0.4 ha) OF SOIL CAN HAVE MORE THAN A MILLION WORMS LIVING IN IT.

Google used a camel *with a* camera mounted on its hump to help map a desert *in the United Arab Emirates.*

SPRAY FROM AFRICA'S VICTORIA FALLS CAN SHOOT 1,600 FEET IN THE AIR. (500 m)

ANCIENT HAWAIIANS SOMETIMES MADE LEIS OUT OF BONES.

EMPEROR PENGUINS CAN'T TASTE THE FISH THEY EAT.

Inventors used a 3-D printer to produce a working electric car.

MARINE SNAILS' TEETH ARE THE STRONGEST MATERIAL FOUND IN NATURE.

Caribou release an odor from their ankles when threatened.

A more than
500-year-
old bed
that may have belonged to
King Henry VII
was recently
found in a
parking lot
in England.

About one-quarter of the world's **hazelnut** supply is used to make **Nutella.**

You can buy a **guitar pick** made from a **meteorite.**

In the United States, more than **20 million tons** (18 million t) of **salt** are spread on snowy roads, parking lots, sidewalks, and driveways each year.

A double somersault with a **TWIST** performed on a trampoline is called a **fliffis.**

Scientists think that **sperm whales** can detect a **swimmer** more than **one mile** (1.6 km) above them.

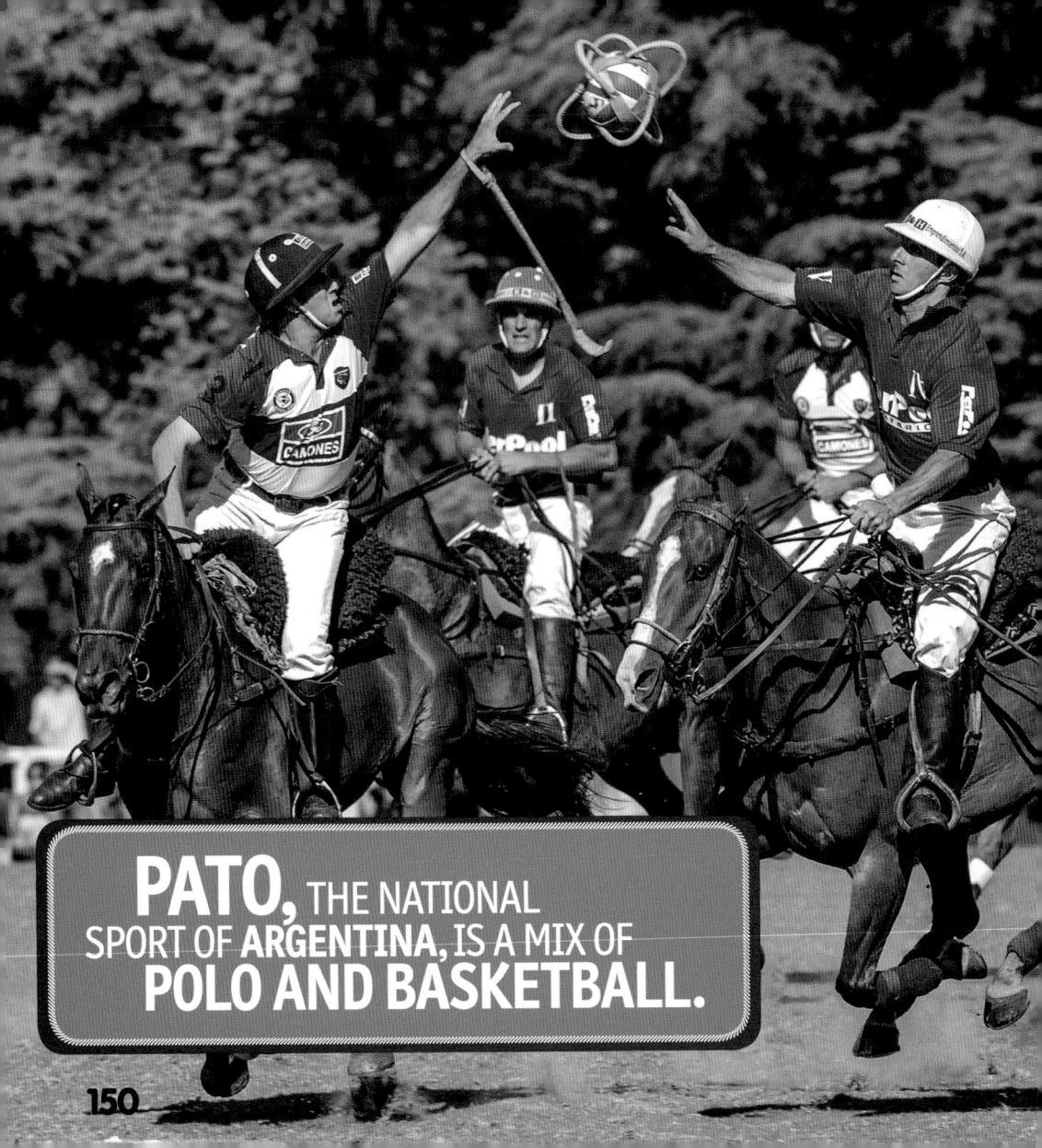

PATO, THE NATIONAL SPORT OF **ARGENTINA,** IS A MIX OF **POLO AND BASKETBALL.**

The average person can recognize about a trillion smells.

The @ symbol is almost five centuries old.

Elizabeth II, Queen of England, served as a mechanic in World War II.

The *Titanic* was held together by 3 million rivets.

CALIFORNIA INVENTORS CREATED

A REAL-LIFE HOVERBOARD.

WATCHING FISH SWIM IN AN AQUARIUM CAN REDUCE STRESS, A STUDY FOUND.

Electric eels can use jolts of electricity to control the muscle movements of the fish they hunt.

YORKSHIRE TERRIER
POODLE

YORKIPOO

THE ISLAND OF MAURITIUS IN THE INDIAN OCEAN HAS MULTICOLORED SAND DUNES.

IN 1808, TWO FRENCHMEN FOUGHT A DUEL WHILE FLOATING IN BALLOONS SOME 2,700 FEET (820 m) ABOVE GROUND.

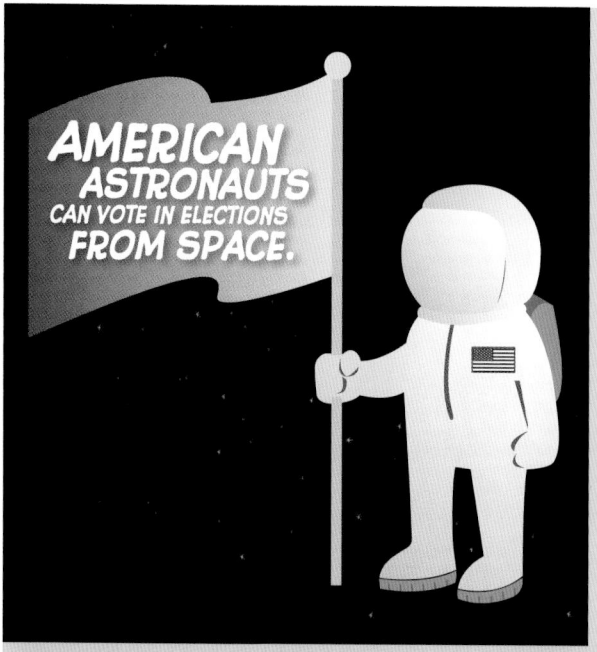

It can take about 25 gallons (95 L) of water to grow one avocado.

The noises Tasmanian devils make when eating can be heard a mile away. (1.6 km)

THE DESERT-DWELLING **FENNEC FOX** HAS HAIRY FOOTPADS THAT PROTECT ITS FEET FROM HOT SAND.

U.S. FAMILIES SPEND AN ESTIMATED **$9 BILLION** ON BACK-TO-SCHOOL **CLOTHES.**

President Gerald Ford once worked as a **park ranger.**

A GROUP OF SHARKS

IS CALLED A SHIVER.

YOU CAN SEE **TRACTOR SQUARE DANCES**— WHERE **FARMERS** MANEUVER TRACTORS TO MIMIC SQUARE DANCING ROUTINES— IN THE MIDWESTERN UNITED STATES.

PEOPLE WHO ARE FREQUENTLY **HUGGED** EXPERIENCE LESS SEVERE **COLD SYMPTOMS**, A STUDY FOUND.

Someone who plays **marbles** is called a **mibster**.

A HAMSTER'S **CHEEK POUCHES** EXTEND ALL THE WAY TO ITS **hips.**

SOME **BOWHEAD WHALES** **LIVE** FOR MORE THAN **200 YEARS.**

LAZE
=
MISTY CLOUDS THAT FORM WHEN HOT LAVA ENTERS THE OCEAN

A study found that the **TEMPERATURE INSIDE OUR CELLS** can reach **122°F** (50°C).

An Italian artist designed a **BATHTUB** shaped like a **HIGH-HEELED SHOE.**

A **TREE** in **CHILE** is called the **MONKEY PUZZLE TREE**— even though **NO MONKEYS** live in the area.

TWO-THIRDS OF AMERICANS use their **FEET** to **FLUSH PUBLIC TOILETS,** according to a survey.

ARCHAEOLOGISTS found a **4,000-year-old "FUNERAL GARDEN"** in Luxor, Egypt, where people may have grown **PLANTS MEANT FOR THE AFTERLIFE.**

AN ARGENTINE opened an ART GALLERY at 14,000 feet (4,300 m) in the **ANDES MOUNTAINS.**

BRIDES who get married in Orlando, Florida, U.S.A., can ride to their wedding in **CINDERELLA'S** GLASS COACH.

A CHINESE NEWSPAPER was once printed on paper made with **500 GRAMS OF GOLD.** (EACH COPY was PRICED at about **$8,100.**)

JAPANESE RESEARCHERS created a material out of gel and fabric that is five times **stronger than carbon steel.**

A VOLCANIC ERUPTION in 1980 caused STREETLIGHTS in some Washington State, U.S.A., cities TO TURN ON IN THE MIDDLE OF THE DAY.

MORE THAN **3,000** YEARS AGO, DECORATED **OSTRICH EGGS WERE TRADED AS LUXURY ITEMS** IN THE **MIDDLE EAST.**

APPLES CAN
RIPEN
TEN TIMES
FASTER
AT ROOM
TEMPERATURE
THAN IN THE
REFRIGERATOR.

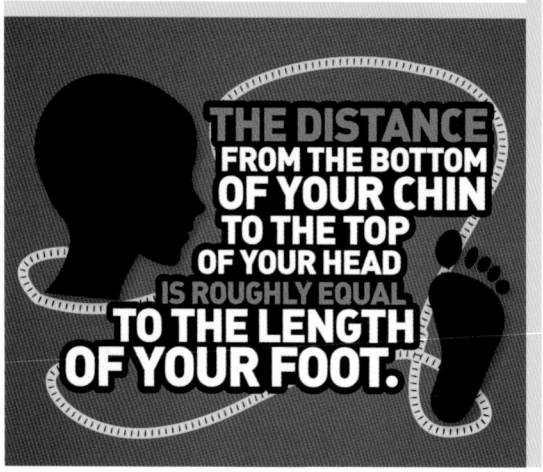
THE DISTANCE
FROM THE BOTTOM
OF YOUR CHIN
TO THE TOP
OF YOUR HEAD
IS ROUGHLY EQUAL
TO THE LENGTH
OF YOUR FOOT.

AT AN
OPERA
HOUSE
ON THE
U.S.–CANADIAN
BORDER,
THE STAGE
IS IN
CANADA WHILE MOST
SEATS
ARE IN THE UNITED
STATES.

One rock in Joshua Tree National Park in California, U.S.A., resembles a giant human skull.

A MALE RED DEER'S ANTLERS CAN GROW

TO A WEIGHT OF 60 POUNDS (27 kg) IN THREE MONTHS.

Six of the seven dwarfs in the 1937 animated movie *Snow White and the Seven Dwarfs* have eyebrows modeled after Walt Disney's.

Temperatures on Mercury can drop more than 1000°F (550°C) in one day.

A PENNY ISSUED BY THE U.S. MINT IN 1793 SOLD AT AUCTION FOR $2.3 MILLION.

The first baseball caps were made from straw.

The most commonly used noun in the English language is "people."
Pelicans can hold more food in their beaks than in their stomachs.
Extreme athletes have skied from the summit of Mount Everest to a base camp 12,000 feet below.
(3,660 m)

ONE ARTIST PAINTED A PICTURE OF BASKETBALL PLAYER YAO MING, USING A BASKETBALL AS A "PAINTBRUSH."
Laid end to end, New York City's subway tracks would stretch from the Big Apple to Chicago, Illinois, U.S.A.

YOU CAN FIND OVER
2,000
ROCK
ARCHES
IN ARCHES NATIONAL PARK,
IN UTAH, U.S.A.

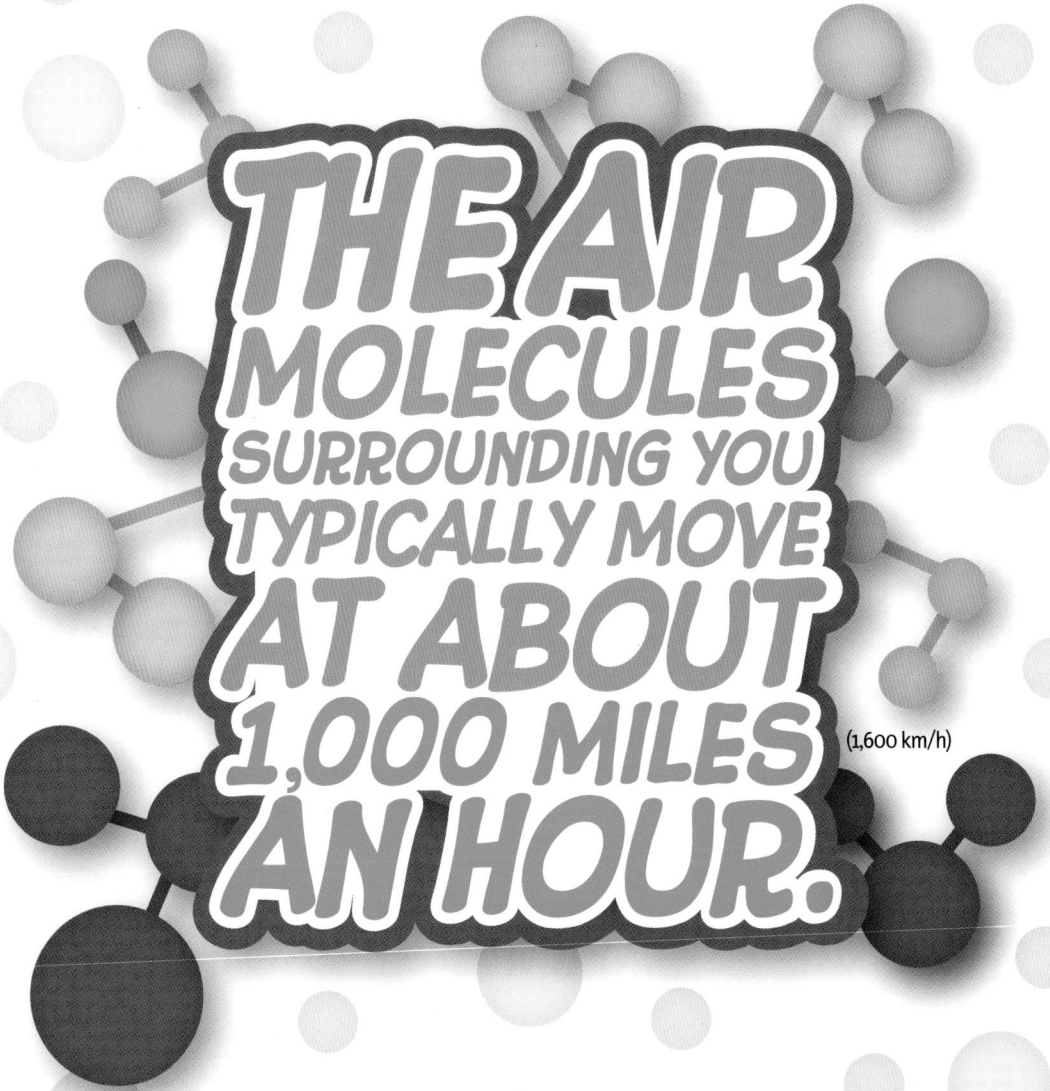
THE AIR MOLECULES SURROUNDING YOU TYPICALLY MOVE AT ABOUT 1,000 MILES AN HOUR.
(1,600 km/h)

BOTTLENOSE DOLPHINS SWALLOW THEIR FOOD WHOLE.

IN JAPAN, KFC GAVE AWAY iPHONE CASES SHAPED LIKE GIANT CHICKEN DRUMSTICKS.

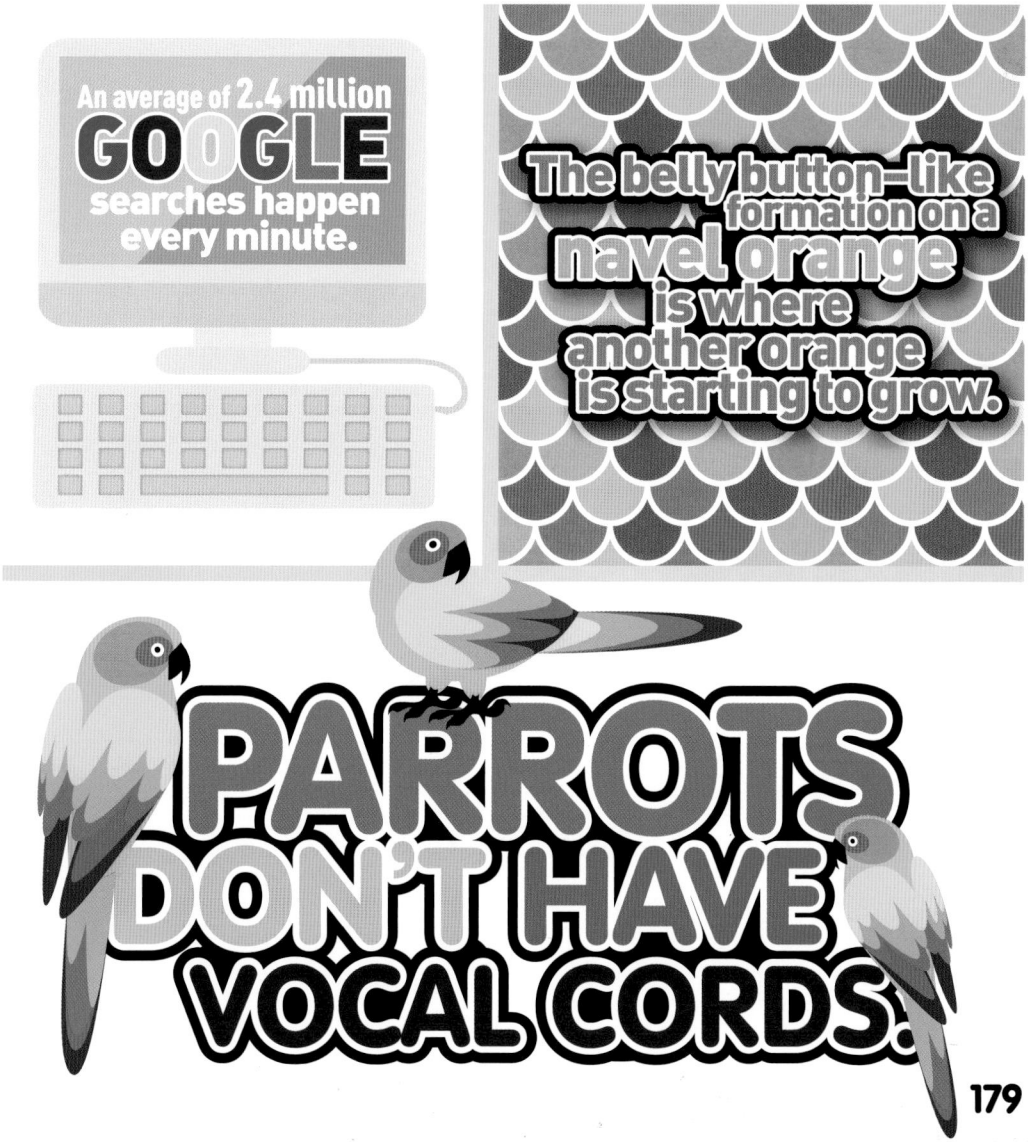
An average of 2.4 million
GOOGLE
searches happen every minute.
The belly button–like formation on a navel orange is where another orange is starting to grow.
PARROTS DON'T HAVE VOCAL CORDS.

A newborn sea otter's extra-thick fur traps in so much air that it's impossible for the animal to sink.

SOME SOCCER BALLS HAVE A BUILT-IN CHIP THAT SIGNALS REFEREES WHEN THE BALL PASSES THE GOAL LINE.

3,240 SOCCER BALLS WERE USED DURING THE 2014 WORLD CUP.

PROFESSIONAL SOCCER PLAYERS RUN AN AVERAGE OF SEVEN MILES (11 km) DURING EACH GAME.

AN INDOOR SOCCER MATCH IN ALBERTA, CANADA, LASTED 30 HOURS AND 10 MINUTES.

AN
ATLANTIC PUFFIN
CAN HOLD
AS MANY AS
A DOZEN
SMALL FISH
IN ITS BILL
AT ONE
TIME.
SOME MOTHS
DON'T HAVE
MOUTHS.

A BILLBOARD IN RIYADH, SAUDI ARABIA, STRETCHES

THE LENGTH OF NEARLY NINE BASKETBALL COURTS.

AN ARTiST IN LONDON, ENGLAND, CONSTRUCTED A BUiLDiNG THAT APPEARS TO LEViTATE.

A HEDGEHOG HAS ABOUT
6,000 QUILLS.

Polar bears sometimes communicate by touching noses.

SOME PEOPLE LACK THE GENE THAT CAUSES SMELLY UNDERARMS.

TRISKAIDEKAPHOBIA IS THE FEAR OF THE NUMBER 13.

THE WORLD'S LARGEST **DISCO BALL** IS MORE THAN **33 FEET** (10 m) IN DIAMETER—ALMOST AS WIDE AS A TENNIS COURT.

The common
octopus
is the
size of a
flea at birth.

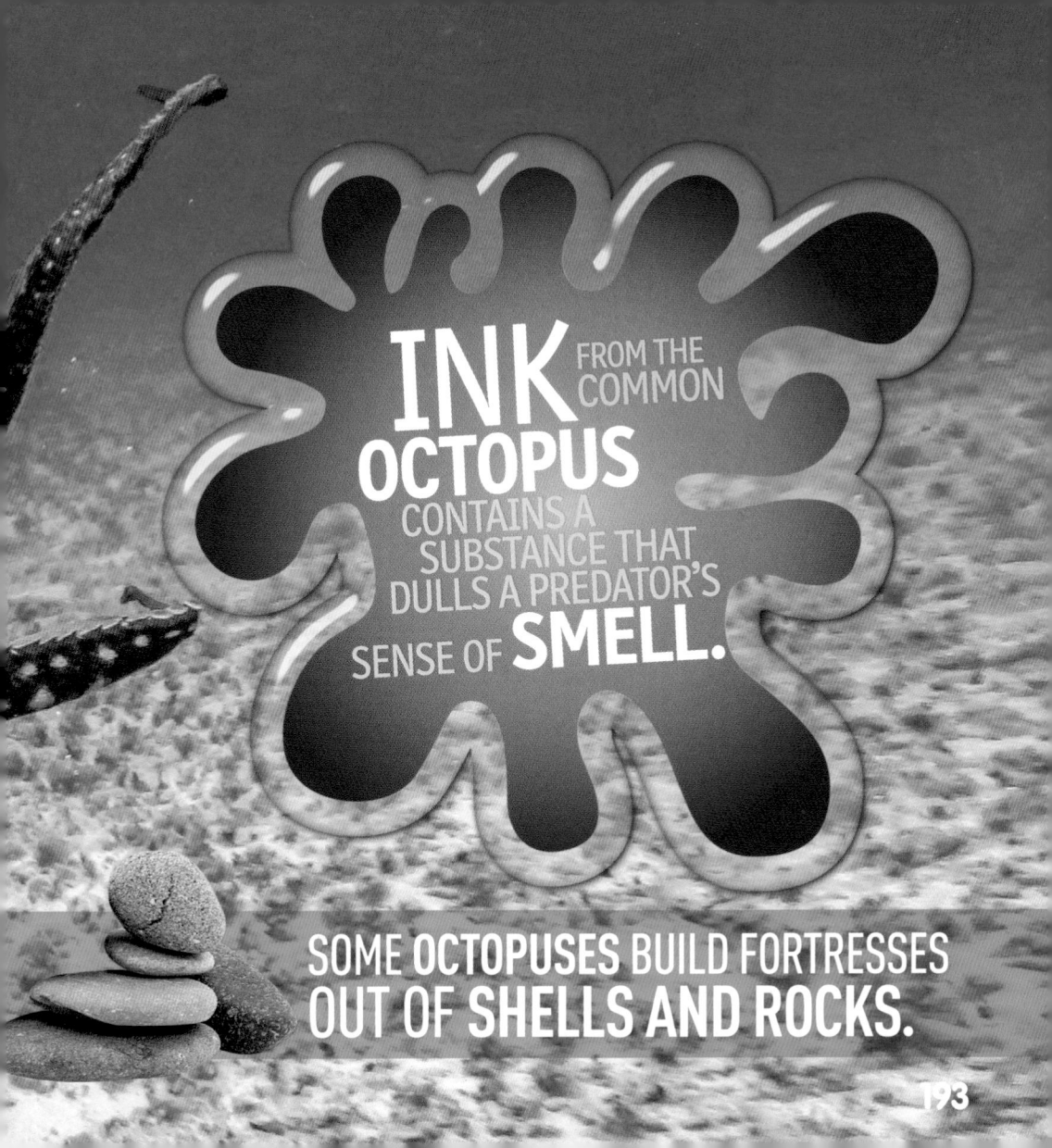
INK FROM THE COMMON OCTOPUS CONTAINS A SUBSTANCE THAT DULLS A PREDATOR'S SENSE OF SMELL.
SOME OCTOPUSES BUILD FORTRESSES OUT OF SHELLS AND ROCKS.

A candy company once made Thanksgiving-themed **gumballs** with flavors such as cranberry, turkey, and pumpkin pie.

SOME **21,000** YEARS AGO, MASSIVE **ICEBERGS** FLOATED OFF THE COAST OF FLORIDA, U.S.A.

Scientists have figured out a way to convert **sugar** into **fuel.**

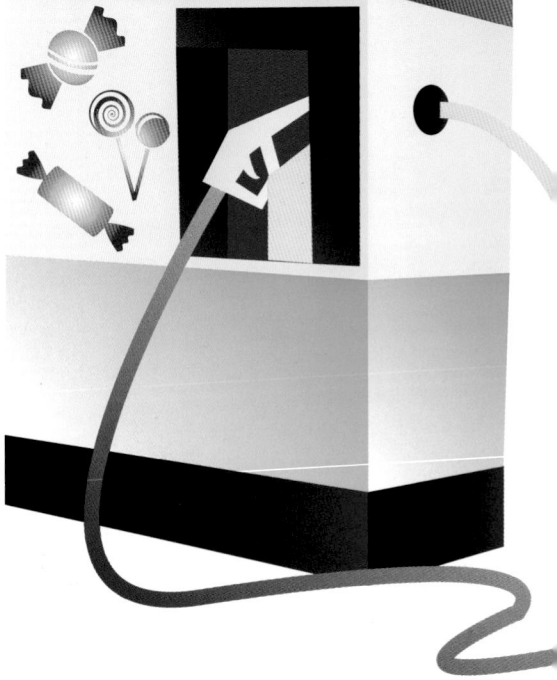

India sent a
spacecraft
known as
MOM
to Mars.

Researchers are trying
to develop a car tire
made from dandelions.

CERTAIN
FERNS
EJECT THEIR
SPORES WITH
A CATAPULT
MOTION.

A GROUP OF GIRAFFES

IS CALLED A TOWER.

Your glabella is the area of skin between your eyebrows.

IN 2014, TWO PROFESSORS LIVED FOR

73 DAYS IN AN AIRTIGHT LODGE

ABOUT **25 FEET** (7.6 m) UNDERWATER

OFF THE COAST OF FLORIDA, U.S.A.

All of Earth's land could fit in the Pacific Ocean.

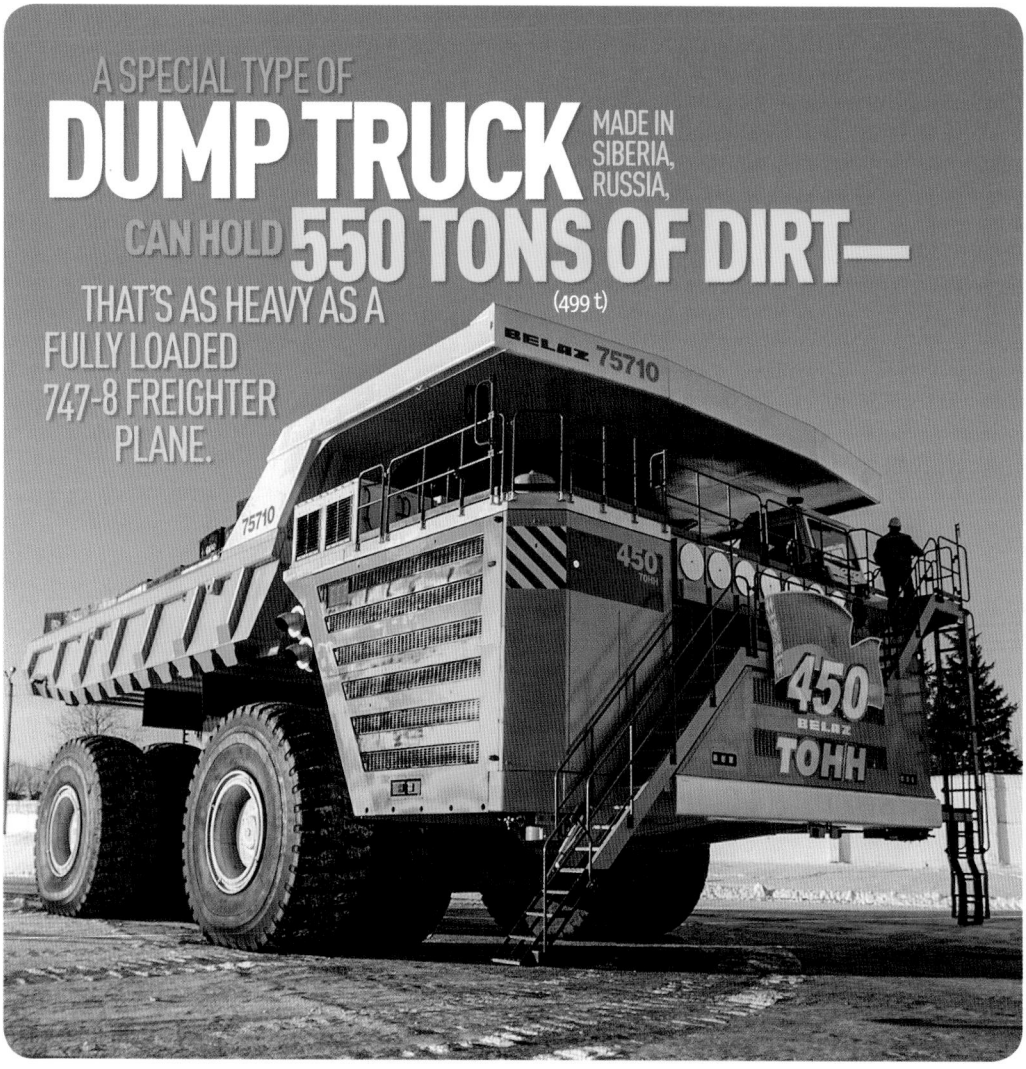
A SPECIAL TYPE OF
DUMP TRUCK
MADE IN SIBERIA, RUSSIA,
CAN HOLD 550 TONS OF DIRT—
(499 t)
THAT'S AS HEAVY AS A FULLY LOADED 747-8 FREIGHTER PLANE.
BELAZ 75710
75710
450
TOHH
450
BELAZ
TOHH

The American goldfinch sometimes sounds as if it's saying "po-tay-toe-chip" when it chirps.

WAVES OFF THE COAST OF PUERTO MALABRIGO, PERU, CAN STRETCH MORE THAN A MILE LONG. (1.6 km)

A SINGLE BANANA IS CALLED A FINGER; A BUNCH IS CALLED A HAND.

MALE KANGAROOS FLEX THEIR BICEPS TO IMPRESS FEMALES.

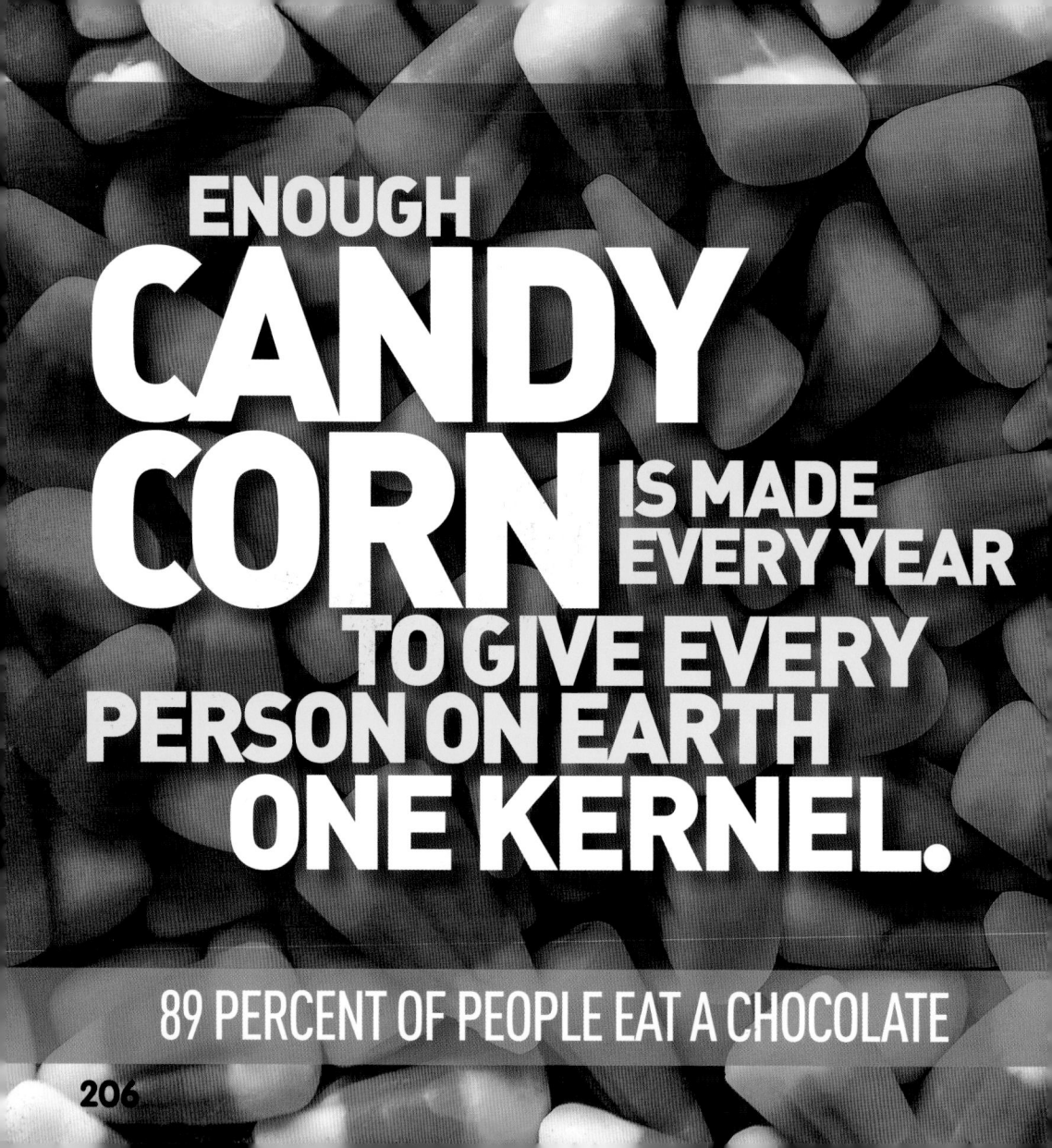
ENOUGH
CANDY
CORN IS MADE
EVERY YEAR
TO GIVE EVERY
PERSON ON EARTH
ONE KERNEL.
89 PERCENT OF PEOPLE EAT A CHOCOLATE

EASTER BUNNY'S EARS FIRST.

GUESS WHAT?

A rainbow that happens at night isn't called a rainbow!

HMM?

Maybe you should be more scared of pigs than sharks!

WHY?

If you wash dishes by hand, you might sneeze less!

WHY?

WANNA FIND OUT?

The FUN doesn't have to end here! Find these far-out facts and more in *Weird But True! 8.*

NATIONAL GEOGRAPHIC KIDS

AVAILABLE WHEREVER BOOKS ARE SOLD

Get a fun freebie at natgeokids.com/fun-pack

© 2018 National Geographic Partners, LLC

FACTFINDER

Boldface indicates illustrations.

A

Air molecules 176
Air travel 14
Airplanes 24, 44, 98–99, **98–99**
Algae 94
Alien life 95
Amazon Basin, South America 48–49, **49,** 77
Andes Mountains, South America 164
Animal groups 66–67, 160–161, 198–199
Antarctica 159
Antlers **134, 168,** 169
Ants 108, **108**
Apples 97, **97,** 166
Arches National Park, Utah, U.S.A. 174, **174–175**
Art
  basketball art 173, **173**
  face masks 65, **65**
  levitating building 186, **186–187**
  wooden hippo 72, **72–73**
Art galleries 164
Astronauts **85,** 158, **158**
@ symbol 151, **151**
Atlantic Ocean 84, **84**
Atlantic puffins 183, **183**
Avocados 158

B

Babies 71, 74, **74**
Bacteria 44
Balloons 157, **157**
Bananas 203, **203**
Baseball 32
Baseball caps **32,** 171
Basketball 69, **69,** 150, 173, **173**
Bathtub, shoe-shaped 164
Bats 90, **90**
Beavers 83, **83**
Beds 146, **146**
Bees 8, 84, **84**
Beeswax 44
Bicycle horns 82
Bicycles 89, **89**
Bike path, glow-in-the-dark 141, **141**
Billboards 184–185
Birds, extinct 39
Blinking 52
Boring, Oregon, U.S.A. 85
Bottlenose dolphins 177, **177**
Bowhead whales 163
Boxers (dogs) 101, **101**
Brain, animal
  cuttlefish 36
  spiders 84
  tarsiers 91
Brain, human 7, **7,** 33
Bread 19, **19,** 96, **96**
Building, levitating 186, **186–187**

C

Camels **48,** 76, **76,** 100, 142, **142–143**
Canada
  doughnut consumption 140
  opera house 166
  polar bear jail 125
Candy canes 207, **207**
Candy corn 206, **206**
Cannonball dives 32
Caribou 145
Cars 88, **88,** 128, 133, 145, **145,** 196
Cashew nuts 134, **134**
Cassowaries 51, **51**
Cats, stress relief for 6
Cauliflower, heaviest 12, **12**
Caves 139
Cedar waxwings 144
Cheese 197, **197**
Chewing gum 14
Chicken Dinner (chocolate bar) 64
Chicken drumsticks 178, **178**
China
  baby-shaped pears 74, **74**
  Ferris wheel 44, **44**
  quartz sunglasses 83

Chocolate 6, **6,** 64, 207, **207**
Christmas Island, Indian Ocean 62, **62**
Churchill, Canada 125
CIA headquarters, Virginia, U.S.A. 59
Cinderella 165
Classical music 27
Clothes, back-to-school 159
Coatis 52, **52**
Cobras 47, **47**
Cockroaches 22, **22**
Coconuts 96
Coffee 114
Coffins **110–111,** 111
Colds 162
Comets 100, **100,** 127
Copenhagen, Denmark 89
Corals and coral reefs 102, **102**
Cosmic dust 107
Couches 6, **6**
Crayola crayons 109, **109**
Cream 84, 114
Crosswalk lights 88, **88**
Cucumbers 112, **112**
Curious George (book) 127
Cuttlefish 36

D

Dandelions 196
Darth Vader 104, **104**
Detroit, Michigan, U.S.A. 141
Disco balls 191, **191**
Disco clams 133
Disney, Walt 170
Divers and diving 32
Diving bell spiders 138, **138**
Dogs
- breeds 154–155, **154–155**
- fastest on hind legs 68, **68**
- fighting 101, **101**
- relaxation 27
- trained to rescue cats 44
- vending machines for 21, **21**

Dollar bills 47
Dolphins 124, **124,** 177, **177**
Doughnuts 45, 68, **68,** 140
Dreadnoughtus (dinosaur) 92, **92–93**
Dreams 56
Drumming 82, **82**
Dubai, United Arab Emirates 88, **88**
Duels 157
Dull, Scotland 85
Dump trucks 202, **202**
Dust storms 124

E

Ears 30
Earth (planet) 13, 44, 124, 201
Earthquakes 63
Earwax 13
Easter chocolate 206–207, **207**
eBay 47
Eggs 24, **24,** 114, **114,** 165
Egypt, ancient 164
Eiffel Tower, Paris, France 139, **139**
Einstein, Albert 82
Electric eels 153
Elizabeth II, Queen (United Kingdom) 151
Ellis Island, New York Bay, U.S.A. 127
Emei mustache toads 144, **144**
Emperor penguins 103, **103,** 145
Empire State Building, New York City, New York **4–5,** 5, **120**
Energy drinks 94
England 8, **60,** 61, 84, 124, 146; *see also* London; Totnes
English (language) 172
Esophagus 13
Everest, Mount, China-Nepal 172
Ewoks 104–105
Exoplanets 45
Eyebrows 170, 200, **200**
Eyelids 33, **33**
Eyes 52, **52,** 82, **82,** 91, **91**

F

Face masks 65, **65**
Fast-food restaurants 20, 124
Fennec foxes 159, **159**

Ferns 197
Ferris wheels 44, **44**
Fish watching 153
Fliffis 147
Fog, toxic 125, **125**
Ford, Gerald 159
Forks 96, **96,** 124
Foxes 159, **159**
Fraser Island, Australia 24
French fries 124, **124**
Frogs 8, 27, **27**
Frorks 124
Fuel 194

G

Gardens **60,** 61, 164
Garlic 190, **190**
Giant cuttlefish 36
Giant pitcher plant 31, **31**
Giraffes 198–199, **198–199**
Glabella 200, **200**
Glow-in-the-dark bike path 141, **141**
Goats 66–67, **66–67,** 97, **97**
Gold 165, 197
Golden orb-weaving spiders 9, **9**
Goldfinches 203, **203**
Golf 97, 116, **116,** 117, **117**
Google 142, 179
Graphite 134–135
Grasshopper Glacier, Montana, U.S.A. 126
Great Barrier Reef, Australia 86, **86–87**
Greece, ancient 85
Guitar picks 147, **147**
Gulf of Mexico 120, **120**
Gumballs 125, 194, **194**

H

Hagfish 81
Hair, human 44
Hamsters 163, **163**
Hawaiians, ancient 145
Hazelnuts 147
Hedgehogs 188, **188**
Hello Kitty 56, **56**
Henry VII, King (England) 146
Hens 114
Hermit crabs 101
Hiking 39
Hippo, wooden **72–73,** 73
The Hobbit (movie trilogy) 25, **25**
Honeybees 8
Honeypot ants 108, **108**
Horses 97
Hotel, snowflake-shaped 28, **28–29**
House: made from waste items 8
Hoverboards 153, **153**
Hubble Space Telescope 140
Hugging 162
Hummingbirds 37, **37**
Hurricanes 53, **53**

I

Ice Age 36
Ice cream 15, **15**
Ice sculptures 126
Icebergs 194
India 77, **77,** 195
Inflatable necklaces 124
Ink, insect-repelling 30
International Space Station 115
Internet 64
iPhone cases 178, **178**

J

Jail, polar bear 125
Japan
doughnuts 68, **68**
iPhone cases 178, **178**
Twitter users 56
Jellyfish 136–137, **136–137**
Joshua Tree National Monument, California, U.S.A. 167, **167**
Jupiter (planet) 126

K

Kangaroos 204–205, **204–205**
Katydids 30, **30**
KELT 11-b (exoplanet) 45
Kepler 413b (planet) 138
KFC 178

L

Larvaceans 45
Laughter 81
Laze (misty clouds) 164, **164**
Leis 145
Leonardo da Vinci 125
Lighthouses 33, **33**
Lightning **4–5,** 5
Lions **2,** 36
Lobsters 80, **80**
London, England 72, **72–73,** 186, **186–187**
Louisiana, U.S.A. 113, **113**
Luxor, Egypt 164

M

Manatees 200, **200**
Manchineel trees 44, **44**
Marbles 162
Marine snails 145
Mars (planet) 124, **124,** 195
Mauritius (island), Indian Ocean 156, **156**
McDonald's 63, **63**
Memory 57
Mercury (planet) 171
Meteorites 147
Mexico 82
Millennium Falcon 105, **105**
Miniature golf 97
Mites 118, **118**
Monkey puzzle trees 164, **164**
Moods 14
Moon 26, **26,** 56, 124
Moose 134
Moths 183, **183**
Mountain lions 33, 128, **128**
Mushrooms 33, **33**
Music 27, 88

N

Naples, Italy 44
National Oreo Day 44
Nectar 31, 108
Nests 75, **75**
Netherlands 96, 141, **141**
Neutron stars 64
New Year's Eve 70
New York City, New York
  artists 114
  doughnuts 45
  New Year's Eve ball 70
  subway 70
  see also Empire State Building; Statue of Liberty
New Zealand
  airport 25, **25**
  diving record 32
  rock formations 34, **34–35**
Newspapers 30, 165
Nile River, Africa 134–135
Nutcrackers 96
Nutella 147

O

Octopuses 192–193, **192–193**
Oklahoma, U.S.A. 185
Onions 190, **190**
Opera houses 166
Oranges 46, **46,** 179
Oreo cookies 44, **44**
Orlando, Florida, U.S.A. 165, **165**
Ospreys 75
Otters **180–181,** 181
Owls **122–123,** 123

P

Pac-Man frogs 27, **27**
Pacific Ocean 201
Pain 138
Parrots 179, **179**
Pasta 44, **44**
Pato (sport) 150, **150**
"Peanuts" comic strips 24
Pears 74, **74**
Pelicans 172, **172**
Pencils 134–135
Penguins 103, **103,** 145
Pennies 171, **171**
Pippi Longstocking 184
Pistol shrimp 94
Pitcher plants 31, **31**
Planets 95
Poison Garden, England **60,** 61
Poison ivy 134, **134**
Polar bears 125, **125,** 189, **189**

Police 140
Police cars 88, **88**
Potato peelers 14, **14**
Pudu (deer) 16, **16–17**
Puffins 183, **183**

Q

Quartz 83, **83**
Queen Mary 2 (ship) 128

R

Races 46, 76, 97
Rainbows 40–41, **40–41**
Ramen noodles 68, **68**
Red crabs 62, **62**
Red deer **168,** 169
Red-footed tortoises 6
Restaurants 20, 75, 84, 124
Rice 52, **52**
Richmond, Virginia, U.S.A. 84
Riyadh, Saudi Arabia 184–185
Robots 32, 103, **103**
Rock formations 34, **34–35,** 167, **167,** 174, **174–175**
Rodents 31, 107
Roman gladiators 94, **94**
Rosemary 85, **85**
Rubik's Cube 130, **130,** 131, **131**

S

Sagada, Philippines **110–111,** 111
Sahara, Africa 48, **48**
Salt 147
Saltwater 128
Sand dunes 156, **156**
Sarcastic fringehead fish **10–11,** 11
Sark Island, English Channel 133
Saturn (planet) 53, **53**
Schulz, Charles M. 24
Sea otters **180–181,** 181
Seattle, Washington, U.S.A. 132, **132**
Sedona, Arizona, U.S.A. 63, **63**
Sewer systems 84, 197, **197**
Sharks 45, **45,** 109, 160, **160–161,** 197
Shoes 119, 164, **164**
Shortfin mako sharks 45, **45**
Shrimp 94, 139
Silver 197
Silver Lake, Colorado, U.S.A. 106
Singapore 124, **124**
Skiing 172
Sleep 43, 56
Sloths 94
Smartshoes 119
Smaug (dragon) 25, **25**
Smell, sense of 193
Snails 145
Snakes 47, **47,** 101
Sneezing 43
Snot 45
Snow 106
Snow White and the Seven Dwarfs (movie) 170
Snowflake-shaped hotel 28, **28–29**
Soccer 182
Solar-energy farm 85, **85**
Spacecraft 38, **38,** 43, **43,** 127, 195
Spaghetti 45, **45**
Sperm whales **148–149,** 149
Spiders 9, **9,** 18, 84, 138, **138**
Sputnik 1 (satellite) 43, **43**
Squat lobsters 80, **80**
Sri Lanka 30
Star dust 125
Star Wars movies 84, 104–105, **104–105**
Starbucks 59
Stars 54–55, **54–55,** 64
Statue of Liberty, New York City, New York 33, **33**
Steam locomotives 97
Stomachs 8, 18, **18,** 172
Stress relief 6, 153
Subway tracks 173, **173**
Sugar 194
Sun 54–55
Sunglasses 83, **83**
Super Soaker water gun 107, **107**
Supreme Court Building, Washington, D.C. 69

T

Tarsiers 91, **91**
Tasmanian devils 158
Taste, sense of 18, 145
Taste buds 128
Teeth 83, **83,** 109, 145
Thanksgiving 194
3-D printing 145
Tianjin Eye, China 44, **44**
Tinkerbell wasps 135
Titanic, R.M.S. (ship) 152, **152**
Toads 144, **144**
Toilet paper rolls 65, **65**
Toilets, public 164
Toothpaste 36, **36,** 109
Tornadoes 185, **185**
Toronto, Canada 84
Tortoises 6, 58, **58**
Totnes, England 46
Touch screens 6
Toxic spills 190
Tractor square dances 162, **162**
Trampolines 147
Treasure, buried 124
Trees: branches 133, **133**
Triskaidekaphobia 190
Trucks 80, **80,** 202, **202**
Tunnels 141
Tut, King (Egypt) 185, **185**
TV stations 50
Twins 140
Twitter 56

U

Ukraine 104
Umbrellas 124, **124**
Underarms 190
United Arab Emirates 142, **142–143**
United States
  Internet use 64
  military 91
  opera house 166
  salt use 147

V

Vending machines 20, **20**
Victoria Falls, Africa 144
Vog 125, **125**
Volcanoes 27, 56, 106, **106,** 124, 125, 165
Voting 158

W

Waffles 114, **114**
Walnut sphinx caterpillars 45
Walruses 78, **78–79**
Walt Disney World 75, **75**
Water 13, 19, **19,** 128, **128,** 158
Water guns 107, **107**
Watermelon seeds 185, **185**
Waves 203
Weight lifting 57
West Indian manatees 200, **200**
Whales **148–149,** 149, 163
Wild pigs 113, **113**
Wind turbines 63, **63**
Wonder Woman 129
Worms 102, **102,** 141

X

X-ray lasers 84

Y

Yao Ming 173, **173**
Yellowstone National Park, U.S.A. 27
Yoda 104
YouTube 42

Z

Zombies 91
Zucchinis 81, **81**

PHOTO CREDITS

SS = Shutterstock

Cover, Eric Isselée/SS; spine, Isselée/Dreamstime;2, Eric Isselée/SS; 4–5, William Anderson/Getty Images; 6 (UP), Courtesy Gugliermetto Experience; 9, Misja Smits, Buiten-beeld/Minden Pictures; 10–11, SeaPics.com; 12, TIG Media/Peter Glazebrook/Caters News Agency; 15, cnicbc/iStockphoto; 16–17, Mark Newman/FLPA/Minden Pictures; 19, Maya Kovacheva Photography/Dreamstime; 21, Yucesan Industries JSC/Rex/REX USA; 22, Antgain/iStock; 23, deamles for sale/SS; 25, Courtesy Weta Workshop; 27, Cristian Batig/Getty Images; 28–29, Architect: Koen Olthuis ñ Waterstudio. NL, Developer: Dutch Docklands; 30, Piotr Naskrecki/Minden Pictures; 31 (LE), Heinrich van den Berg/Getty Images; 31 (UP RT), Schankz/SS; 31 (LO RT), Henrik Larsson/SS; 32 (UP), Brashest/SS; 33, George McCarthy/Nature Picture Library; 34–35, Raimund Linke/Getty Images; 34, Christi Tolbert/SS; 37, Evgeniya Uvarova/SS; 40–41, AP Photo/David Goldman; 43 (UP), subjug/iStock; 43 (LO), NASA/Asif A. Siddiqi; 44 (UP LE), CKP1001/SS; 44 (UP RT), Darryl Brooks/SS; 44 (CTR), thatreec/SS; 44 (LO), yingtustocker/SS; 45 (UP), nfmlk/SS; 45 (LO), Richard Herrmann/Minden Pictures; 47, Eric Isselée/SS; 48, Cyril Ruoso/Minden Pictures; 49, Kevin Schafer/Minden Pictures; 51, Kevin Schafer/Minden Pictures; 52, James Hager/Robert Harding World Imagery/Corbis; 53, NASA/JPL-Caltech/SSI/Hampton University; 54–55, Illustration courtesy Gabriel Perez Diaz, Instituto de Astrofisica de Canarias; 58, Tui De Roy/Minden Pictures; 60, Rick Strange/Alamy; 61, Rosa Betancourt/0 people images/Alamy; 62, Stephen Belcher/Minden Pictures; 63, MWA/ZOJ/Michael Wright/WENN.com/Newscom; 64, Miketanct/iStockphoto; 65, Courtesy Oznoon by Junior Fritz Jacquet/CFSE AGAPE ART; 66–67, Margot Kessler/iStock; 68, David Livingston/Getty Images; 72–73, Joe Alvarez; 74, Europics/Newscom; 75, Elenazarubina/Dreamstime; 76, Al Shibla/Caters News Agency; 77, AridOcean/SS; 78–79, Paul Nicklen/National Geographic Creative; 80 (LE), Chris Newbert/Minden Pictures; 80 (RT), Photo courtesy of Rick Sullivan; 83 (LE), Aprescindere/Dreamstime; 83 (RT), maman/SS; 84 (LE), William Bradberry/SS; 84 (RT), Valentin Volkov/SS; 84 (LO), maodoltee/SS; 85 (bees), nejumi/SS; 85 (UP), domnitsky/SS; 85 (LE), PETIT Philippe/Getty Images; 85 (RT), Dmitry Simin/SS; 86–87, ltos/iStock; 88, The Asahi Shimbun/Getty Images; 91, Edwin Verin/Dreamstime; 92–93, Illustrator, Jennifer Hall/Courtesy Carnegie Museum; 96, Courtesy HapiFork; 97, Iman Khalili; 98–99, Melanie Stetson Freeman/The Christian Science Monitor/Getty Images; 100, NASA; 102, Chris Newbert/Minden Pictures; 103, Newscom; 104, Lucasfilm/Sunset Boulevard/Corbis/Getty Images; 105 (UP LE), Courtesy of Olivier C.; 105 (CTR), Susana Vera/Reuters; 105 (LO RT), Lucasfilm Ltd./Everett Collection; 106, Olivier Grunewald; 108, Reg Morrison/Auscape/Minden Pictures; 110–111, Christian Kober/Robert Harding World Imagery; 113, Imagebroker RF/Getty Images; 114, Chris Dimino, Designer; 116, shirophoto/iStock; 117 (BACK), Andresrimaging/iStock; 117 (LO), Steve Allen/SS; 119 (footprints), Panptys/SS; 120 (LE), NASA; 120 (RT), Pedre/iStockphoto; 121, Gallo Images/Alamy; 122–123, Martin Willis/Minden Pictures; 124 (UP LE), NASA; 124 (UP RT), nano vector/SS; 124 (LO LE), Olaf Schuelke/Alamy Stock Photo; 124 (LO RT), Igor Zh./SS; 125 (UP LE), aquariagirl1970/SS; 125 (UP RT), LMspencer/SS; 125 (LO RT), Eric Isselée/Dreamstime; 126, somchaij/SS; 128, Dean Pennala/SS; 130, guroldinneden/iStockphoto; 131, Courtesy Oskar Van Deventer; 132, Peregrine Church/Rainworks; 136–137, Jorg Hackemann/SS; 138, Stephen Dalton/Nature Picture Library; 141, Daan Roosegaarde; 143, Courtesy Google Maps; 144, ChinaFotoPress/Getty Images; 145, Courtesy Local Motors Inc./Nyko de Peyer; 146 (BACK), Sakarin Sawasdinaka/SS; 146 (FRONT), Courtesy The Langley Collection; 147, Viktorfischer/Dreamstime; 148–149, Jens Kuhfs/Getty Images; 150, Eduardo Mariano Rivero/Alamy; 153, Arx Pax; 154 (LE), GlobalP/iStock; 154 (RT), vitcom/iStock; 155, Chrystal Moore/Alamy; 156, Oleg Znamenskiy/SS; 159 (UP), Photononstop RM/Getty Images; 159 (LO), Lucky-photographer/SS; 160–161, bradlifestyle/SS; 162, EPA/Chris Gardner/Newscom; 163, Juniors Bildarchiv GmbH/Alamy; 164 (UP LE), Allen.G/SS; 164 (UP RT), AveNa/SS; 164 (CTR), Andrew/SS; 164 (LO LE), Sergio Bob/SS; 165 (UP), Rodrigo Varela/Getty Images; 165 (LO), Aaron Amat/SS; 167, Lunamarina/Dreamstime; 168, Mark Raycroft/Minden Pictures; 171, AP Photo/Heritage Auctions; 173, Courtesy "Red" Hong Yi; 174–175, Flickr RF/Getty Images; 177, UIG/Getty Images; 178 (LE), Courtesy YUM! Brands; 178 (RT), Courtesy YUM! Brands; 180–181, Donald M. Jones/Minden Pictures; 183, David Robertson/Alamy; 187, Covent Garden Piazza, London - Artist, Alex Chinneck/photographer, Jeff Moore; 188, American Images Inc/SuperStock; 191, Victor Frankowski/REX/Newscom; 192–193, OceanBodhi/iStockphoto; 193 (LO), diosmic/iStockphoto; 198–199, Oleg Znamenskiy/SS; 200, Jeff Mondragon/Alamy; 202, www.siemens.com/press; 204–205, Dave Watts/Alamy; 206–207 (BACKGROUND), Pierre Leclerc/Dreamstime; 207 (LE), Kitano/Dreamstime; 207 (RT), Richard Cote/Dreamstime

Copyright © 2015 National Geographic Society
Copyright © 2018 National Geographic Partners, LLC

Published by National Geographic Partners, LLC. All rights reserved. Reproduction of the whole or any part of the contents without written permission from the publisher is prohibited.

Since 1888, the National Geographic Society has funded more than 12,000 research, exploration, and preservation projects around the world. The Society receives funds from National Geographic Partners, LLC, funded in part by your purchase. A portion of the proceeds from this book supports this vital work. To learn more, visit natgeo.com/info.

NATIONAL GEOGRAPHIC and Yellow Border Design are trademarks of the National Geographic Society, used under license.

For more information, visit nationalgeographic.com, call 1-800-647-5463, or write to the following address:
National Geographic Partners
1145 17th Street N.W.
Washington, D.C. 20036-4688 U.S.A.

Visit us online at nationalgeographic.com/books

For librarians and teachers:
ngchildrensbooks.org

More for kids from National Geographic:
natgeokids.com

For information about special discounts for bulk purchases, please contact National Geographic Books Special Sales:
specialsales@natgeo.com

For rights or permissions inquiries, please contact National Geographic Books Subsidiary Rights: bookrights@natgeo.com

Designed by Rachel Hamm Plett, Moduza Design

First edition published 2015
Reissued and updated 2018

Trade paperback ISBN: 978-1-4263-3116-9
Reinforced library binding ISBN:
978-1-4263-3117-6

The publisher would like to thank Jen Agresta, project manager; Michelle Harris, researcher; Andrea Silen, project editor; Paige Towler, project editor; Julide Dengel, art director; Kathryn Robbins, art director; Ruthie Thompson, designer; Lori Epstein, photo director; Hillary Leo, photo editor; Joan Gossett, production editor; Gus Tello and Anne LeongSon, production assistants.

Printed in China
18/PPS/1